POWER

POSZ

POWER POSZ

AND OTHER HACKS FOR GETTING THE JOB YOU WANT

PAMELA POSZ

Printed in the United States of America

First Printing, 2020

ISBN 978-1-735-51790-2

Be yourself; everyone else is already taken.

OSCAR WILDE

Everyone wants to live on top of the mountain, but all the happiness and growth occurs while you're climbing it.

ANDY ROONEY

Contents

Introduction

Welcome to This Book

You'll find all of the information you need, and hopefully much more, to get the job you want.

Why Have I Written This Book?

I wrote this book because though many of us have pursued training and education in order to do a job, most people have received little to no training on how to get the job. This was certainly my experience. Nowhere in my college career did a receive training on how to find, apply for, and attain positions I was interested in. I was successful because I was lucky, payed attention, and had a good network. Hopefully this book can help those of you who don't have help to give you the information you need in order to be successful in your job search.

Why Should You Listen to My Advice?

I know a lot about how to find, apply to, and get the job you want. I've figured out a variety of hacks that are really useful when you're looking for a job.

I wasn't always an expert in this area. I'm a librarian and it's what I've been doing for my entire career. It's a great profession and I love it. But when I started my career, I was as clueless as anyone else who buys a job search book. I picked up tips here and there and often was hired for positions because I seemed to do well with the application and the interview. But my real inspiration for this book started when I started teaching a job searching class. I started to subscribe to newsletters and websites about getting a job. I started to really follow the resources in this area. And I picked up a lot of information that many don't seem to know.

For several years I've been teaching my students, and anyone else who will listen, about how to find jobs, write resumes, network, interview and other skills, techniques and strategies that are useful when you are looking for a job. I've observed that in general, people aren't familiar with much of this information and are unsurprisingly, extremely stressed about everything relating to looking for a job. However, I have found that when I have provided individuals with any of the information in this book, they have understood the job-hunting process much better, have done better, and have often got the job they wanted.

Job hunting is one of the most stressful experiences that you will have. The stakes are extremely high and most people don't seem to be sure about what they need to do to be successful. The process seems rigid and mysterious all in one. There seem to be a lot of unwritten rules that you may not understand. There are many rules but no rulebook.

All of this adds up to a huge amount of stress for almost anyone who is looking for a job.

I've written this book to provide practical information and tips that I hope will be useful to you and will reduce your stress about looking for a job.

Why Have You Bought This Book?

You have a job interview tomorrow. Great. You'll find a short list of things you can do to prep for the job tonight. **Go to Chapter 5 and then come back and read the rest of the book later.**

You've never looked for a job before. Great. This book will walk you through the entire process from Analyzing the Job Advertisement (Section 1.4) to Resumes and Cover Letters (Chapter 3) to Interviewing (Chapter 4) to thank you notes (Section 3.10). It's the whole package. I've tried to create the kitchen sink of job-hunting books.

You've applied for a bunch of jobs and aren't getting any interviews. The problem is probably your application or your resume (Chapter 3).

Make a few of the tweaks I suggest and see what happens.

You've applied for a bunch of jobs. You get an interview but you are never offered a job. Go straight to the Interviewing section (Chapter 4) for some practical tips and tricks.

Have another reason I didn't mention? Great. Read the rest of the book and see what else you learn.

Caveats

I'm an expert but I don't know everything. Although I know quite a bit about this topic, there are areas where my advice may not hold true, particularly if the rules in a specific field (graphic design, auto repair, theater, etc.) are different than what I've observed. If you know that your field does things differently, go with what you know works in your field. For example, if you are trying to get a job in a theater and you know that the resume format is different than what I've discussed, go with the format you know works for theater jobs. However, I'd still recommend skimming the resume section because most of the suggestions will work for any job application. Most of the advice in this book will work for the majority of those looking for a job regardless of your field of interest.

This book will be useful for anyone who is looking for a job. However, you may notice a few ways in which I focus the information.

Much of the information is tailored to anyone looking for a public sector job. The public sector jobs are those where you'll be working for a government agency or organization. The field of education also falls into this category. This is in contrast to private sector jobs where you'd be working for a company. The advice in this book primarily applies to the public sector, although some of the concepts are true regardless of which direction you go. This is particularly true for the hiring process. In terms of hiring, non-profit more closely resembles the private sector than the public sector.

As you read the book you may also notice that there is a focus on information relating to looking for a job in California. I live and work in Northern California and I'm more familiar with this geographic region and the relevant resources that are local. However, you should be able to find equivalent resources in your area of the country. For example, in the Information Resources chapter, many of the websites are specific to California. You should be able to find other similar websites in your region.

And finally, there is also a focus on the library profession. Many of the examples are library examples. I am a librarian and the class I teach is Library Job Hunting Skills. Most of the examples will relate to my profession. However, much of the information is general enough to be useful to anyone.

Networking Strikes Again

Professional networking as an essential skill for your job hunt.

Throughout this book I'll insert this symbol and this phrase, Networking Strikes Again, to indicate another area where networking will be useful.

Hopefully this will help you understand all of the areas where networking can play a critical role in your job search.

You'll find the main discussion of networking in Chapter 2.

Why Are There Silly Bits and Pet Photos?

Job hunting is stressful enough. If this book can help you de-stress in any way, I'll consider that to be a positive outcome.

Chapter 1 – General Advice

1.1 Where to Find Jobs and Other Useful Information Resources

Before we go into the many topics I cover in this book, let's look at useful resources for your job search.

This list includes the resources I've found to be particularly useful.

As with any other information, some of the sources in this book will be instantly out of date. However, I've tried to include resources that have been around for a while and are less likely to disappear by the time you read this book.

Books

There are almost an infinite number of job–hunting books on the market at any given time (including this one). I like to use print books because I can mark the pages that are useful (if it's not a library book). These are a few that I've found to be useful for job hunting.

• *What Color is Your Parachute?* by Richard N. Bolles

This is the grandmother of all job hunting books that has been around since the 1970s. It contains quite a bit of good advice for anyone who's looking for a job.

There's a reason it's still very popular. A new edition is published every year and there are different versions for different types of job seekers, such as teens and retirees.

• *Banish Your Inner Critic: Silence the Voice of Self–Doubt to Unleash Your Creativity and Do Your Best Work* by Denise Jacobs

This may seem to be a bit of a strange recommendation given that looking for a job may not seem to be the most creative of endeavors. However, it's been my observation that people (particularly women) have a hard time broadcasting their strengths and abilities,

5

i.e. what they're awesome at. This book provides exercises for determining your strengths that will allow you to silence your inner critic, put your best self forward, and get out of your own way; all of which are critical skills when you're looking for a job. I highly recommend it. I have completely highlighted my own copy and wouldn't want to lend it out, it's that good!

Networking Books (see section 2.1 for why they're relevant)

• *How to Talk to Anyone: 92 Little Tricks for Big Success in Relationships* by Leil Lowdnes

• *Networking for People Who Hate Networking: A Field Guide for Introverts, the Overwhelmed, and the Underconnected* by Devorah Zack

• *Work the Pond* by Darcy Rezac

Websites and Apps

Networking Websites

• **Glassdoor** – http://www.glassdoor.com

This is another big professional networking site. It's a good place to search for inside information about a company. There's an app available.

• **LinkedIn** – https://www.linkedin.com

This is the professional version of Facebook and the biggest professional networking website.

If you are looking for a job it is essential that you have a LinkedIn profile.

Even if you aren't actively looking for a job, LinkedIn is the best way to maintain your professional network.

You'll find more information about LinkedIn in section 2.2.

There's an app available.

- **Twitter** – https://twitter.com

Twitter can be very useful for your job hunt. Companies and organizations post positions, people post advice, you can follow trends in your industry and network with individuals you might not usually have contact with. You do need to create an account to truly make use of twitter. Obviously, there is an app.

General Job–Hunting Websites and Apps

Many job websites offer an email notification option. You will receive email notifications about new job postings as they are added to the website based on criteria that you enter such as distance and job title.

The apps also offer similarly useful features.

- **CareerBuilder** – http://www.careerbuilder.com

An app is available.

- **Careerealism** – http://www.careerealism.com

Their slogan is "Because every job is temporary." A comprehensive website of job–hunting resources with good specific advice about job hunting.

- **EdJoin.org** – http://www.edjoin.org

This is particularly good for finding jobs in the education field. If you are looking for a job in a school, you should sign up for notifications of new job listings from this website.

They will send you email when new material is posted.

An app is available.

- **GovernmentJobs.com** – https://www.governmentjobs.com

Another location to find federal, state and local government jobs.

- **HERC – The Higher Education Recruitment Consortium –** http://www.hercjobs.org

I subscribe to the HERC JobSeeker SmartBrief and receive regular emails about effective ways to do activities such as informational interviews, cover letters, and other relevant information.

- **HigherEdJobs** – http://www.higheredjobs.com

One of the best sources for jobs in higher education, i.e. colleges and universities.

- **Indeed** – http://www.indeed.com

Their slogan is "one search. all jobs." An app is available.

- **Mock Questions** – https://www.mockquestions.com

This is an excellent website for finding interview questions from different fields.

- **Monster.com** – http://www.monster.com

An app is available.

- **The Muse** – https://www.themuse.com

You can search for jobs on this website. It's particularly useful for career advice and worth signing up for the daily email if you are looking for a job.

- **Simply Hired** – http://www.simplyhired.com

Another source for job alerts. There's an app available.

- **SnagAJob** – http://www.snagajob.com

Another source for job alerts. An app is available.

- **USAJobs** – https://www.usajobs.gov

This is the Federal government's official job list.

You can search for U.S. government jobs throughout the United States and overseas.

- **Vitae** – https://chroniclevitae.com

This is a website for those in academia that is hosted by the Chronicle of Higher Education. You can search for jobs, get advice and find other relevant information relating to any career in higher education.

California Specific Job-Hunting Websites

I live in California so I am familiar with the California specific job-hunting websites, which is why I'm posting these.

Many of the websites that are specific to California will have a local equivalent if you are living in another state.

For example, each state should have a centralized website where you can find all of the state jobs.

There should also be a website where you can search for city and county jobs.

- **CalJOBS** – https://www.jobs.ca.gov

This is the site to find and apply for jobs with the state of California. The application is not easy and will take some time to fill out correctly. Other states should have similar websites.

- **CalOpps** – https://www.calopps.org

This is one of the best sources for local California government jobs, such as city and county jobs.

For example, this would be one of the best places to start if you were looking for a public library job.

College and University Career Information

College and universities provide a variety of career services to their students and alumni. However, much of the information is accessible even if you aren't a student at that school and can be invaluable to any job seeker.

If you are a student at a college or university, use the career services that are available to you as a student. If you are currently enrolled, start to work on your job hunt before you graduate. If you have graduated and still live in the same area where you went to school, use the career services that are available to you as an alumnus of your college or university. This is particularly important in terms of networking. Fellow alumni will often go out of their way to help graduates from the same school. There are also special opportunities for students and alumni. For example, colleges and universities will often organize networking events for current and former students. These are excellent networking opportunities and may be somewhat less intimidating than a general community networking event since you'll already have something in common with your fellow attendees.

If you aren't living near your alma mater, you should check out what is available at local colleges and universities. For example, I graduated from the Library School at the University of Illinois but I live in Northern California. The closest local library school is the iSchool at San Jose. They have a Career Development website (http://ischool.sjsu.edu/career-development) with a large amount of publicly available information. If I were looking for a job, I would definitely use any local job-hunting websites of this variety.

Professional Organizations

Professional organizations (both national and local) are an important part of any job hunt.

Many of them have useful career centers with places to find jobs, post resumes and find a variety of useful information about finding a job and preparing for the job market.

Placement Agencies

Placement agencies are organizations that connect job seekers to employers. I would recommend trying to find a specific placement agency that works in the field in which you wish to become employed. For example, if you're a scientist, you should try to connect to a placement agency that works with scientific employers.

Now let's look at a few basics to keep in mind for your job search.

1.2 The Basics

Before we go into specific tips and tricks that will really help you get the job you want, let's discuss a few general strategies and techniques that apply to everything in your job search. These are things you should keep in mind throughout the process.

Think of Your Job Hunt as a Game

Searching for a job is one of the most stressful activities you'll participate in. This is because it's extremely important and it will have a long-term impact on many parts of your life ranging from income level to general life satisfaction. I want you to be successful in your job search and so one of my goals with this book is to reduce your stress levels. I'll talk about it in several areas and section 4.7 covers stress reduction tips.

As general way to reduce your stress with the entire process, I've found that it can help to reframe the job search as a game. This doesn't mean that you shouldn't take it seriously. However, there's a lot of research showing the benefits of thinking about activities as games.

People tend to persist more and feel better if you can think about something as a game. To truly understand this concept, I'd recommend watching the 2012 TED talk by Jane McGonigal "The Game that Can Give You 10 Extra Years of Life."[1] It's a great talk and there are other specific ideas you might find useful.

Soft Skills Will Get You the Job

Hard skills, such as your knowledge of how to use a word processor or create a spreadsheet will prepare you for work. But it's the soft skills, such as your ability and willingness to network, that will get you the job.

What Do You Have to Offer?

What are the top five qualities about yourself that you want to convey?

Decide on these qualities as a first step and use them to tell a story about yourself throughout the job-hunting process. You'll find it easier to sell yourself.

Here are a few you might want to consider:

- Technology skills
- People skills
- Adaptability
- Attention to Detail
- Comfort and enjoyment of a diverse work environment
- Creativity

You should also think about how you can meet the needs of your future employer. What can you do for them?

Demonstrate Technology Skills

Technology skills are important for almost any job. Include and emphasize your technology skills throughout the job-hunting process.

Equity

For public sector jobs, one of the most important concepts to understand is that all applicants must be treated equitably.

Most public agencies go to great lengths to ensure that the process is equitable and fair to all candidates.

As much as possible, the application process must be the same for each applicant. This includes the whole process, from application screening to interviewing.

In practical terms, the effect of equity on the hiring process is that it is more bureaucratic and rule driven than you might find in the private sector.

This also means that if you don't correctly submit your application, the agency won't track you down. You will simply be screened out.

I'll discuss this more in later sections.

You Will Have Many Jobs

Don't assume that your first job you will be the job you'll want to stay with for the rest of your life. It often takes people a while to find a job they love.

Remember that you're building a set of experiences that you can draw on for later positions.

If you're in a temporary job, you should still be looking for something permanent.

Always move forward and keep looking, until you have the job you love.

Job Hunting Is Like Dating

Job hunting is one of the most important activities you'll participate in. In many ways it parallels dating. Self–confidence is really important. You will do better in an interview when you feel confident about yourself.

Quick Tips

Look at other people's profiles to see how you stack up. See how other people phrase things.

For any materials you create such as application, resume and cover letter. Write the documents and then put them away. Pull them out again after a little bit to review them again.

Start working on all of your materials well in advance of when you need them. You don't want to be rushed when creating anything.

If possible, for non-native English speakers, try to find a native English speaker to look at all of your materials before you submit them.

Be Prepared for Bureaucracy

The application and interview process for public sector jobs may seem to be even more stressful because the process seems to be more bureaucratic with more rules and barriers. The way hiring is done is somewhat different between the public sector and the private sector however, there are still things that can improve your chances.

There is usually a fairly high level of bureaucracy and there are strict processes that govern everything.

Following instructions to the letter is extremely important and can make or break your ability to get hired.

For example, if you don't fill out the application correctly, you may be screened out at the first level, regardless of how impressive your resume is. For example, in many libraries, librarians and other library staff do not have direct control over the hiring process, although they will help with the decision about who is to be hired. The hiring process is often run through Human Resources, either at the city/county level, or for some larger library locations, at a central library HR department. Up until the actual job interview, you may either be dealing with HR staff or library staff without knowing which is which.

Keep this in mind with your application materials and be aware that people outside your field may not understand the jargon and procedures that are second nature to you.

1.3 Study Up Butter Cup – Do Your Research

One of the keys to success in your job hunt is preparation and practice. In order to be able to practice and prepare, you'll need to do some research about the field or type of work, about the company or organization and the people who work there, and about the specific position.

There's a fair amount of fairly easy research that you be part of the process when you apply for a job.

Even a small amount of research, can greatly increase your chances of getting the job.

Research sets you up for success with the job interview. For example, you can ask specific questions about the organization during your interview. You can mention examples from your work history that match the work at the organization. You can use the correct language and vocabulary in your application and interview answers. You can learn basic information and details, such as details about technology, that will greatly strengthen your interview answers.

It gives you a huge advantage when you interview. If you've done your research and can articulate this in the interview, it indicates that you are familiar with and want to work for that specific organization rather than that you're simply applying for any job. It's one of the major qualities that employers are looking for in a job interview.

If you aren't sure how to do the research or would like a little help, visit your local library. The librarian will be happy to help you.

Start With the Job Advertisement

Study the job ad for clues about questions you may be asked. Look at section 1.4 for an in-depth explanation about how to do that.

16

Check Out the Website

Delve into the website for the organization. Review the entire website. Find the mission statement. Look for policies.

Find the names of staff members and then search for them. Use LinkedIn to see who they're connected to and research any other names you find.

Look for materials that staff members may have published. Look for any awards they may have won. Are there any projects they are working on? Really go through the entire website. You'll find a wealth of information without a huge amount of effort.

Use the Interwebs

It's really easy to Google the organization to see the general information on the Internet. Additionally, if the organization isn't doing well or is an unpleasant place to work, this should be apparent with a quick Google search.

Just make sure you have the right organization. If the name is common, you need to make sure it's the specific organization you want to work for.

Google the job title and see what sort of information comes up. Look for unfamiliar vocabulary and search for it.

Utilize social media too. Search for individuals and organizations and follow them.

Use social media such as Twitter and Facebook to see what's trending. Do a general search to find people who seem to be knowledgeable and/or well connected, look at what they've posted and follow them if it interests you and if it's possible.

Networking Strikes Again – Inside Research

Researching a position and company is also an area where your professional network can be invaluable. If you know of anyone in this type of position or the field, pick their brain. Ask them if they know anything about the organization. Are there any trends you might want to know about? Any specific details they can provide about the organization and interview process? Is it a good place to work?

If you actually know someone who's working at that organization it's even better, a gold–mine of information. You can find out if there's an inside candidate, what the organization is specifically looking for, what interview questions might be asked, how you should dress for an interview, and much more.

What's Current?

Are you worried that you may be hit with an interview question that you lack the knowledge for? You may have missed that class in school or it may even have been a while since you were in school.

There could also easily be a new trend or technology that you are unfamiliar with, particularly if your field evolves rapidly.

One of the best options to see what is really current in a field is to try to track down conference programs and proceedings. Conferences are where people discuss the most recent advances in their field. They are the best place to find out what's really current. It's not hard to find the conference programs online. You can also look for conference proceedings. They will provide more details about specific conference sessions. Look for national, local, and conferences for specific subject areas.

1.4 Analyzing the Job – Visual Version

How to Analyze a Job Advertisement

For this section, I'll go through how I'd analyze a job advertisement description or advertisement the way that I would if I were going to apply for that position.

Demonstrating that you have done your homework about the job for which you are applying in your application materials and later in an interview (if you get one) will greatly improve your chances of getting the job.

I've chosen a general child care position as an example, but you would go through this process for any job for which you are applying.

Obviously for this position you would need to know about early childhood education and specifics of working in a childcare environment.

Step 1: Save and possibly print a copy of the ad. You'll want to refer back to it while you're completing your application, resume, and cover letter, and additionally when you prepare for the interview.

Step 2: Circle or highlight important words from the ad. You'll focus on these in your application.

Step 3: Make sure that you use the language from the ad in your application materials. For example, this ad uses the phrase "mentor and direct" (item 1h). You would use that exact phrase in your application, resume, and cover letter to describe your experience.

Step 4: Decide the more generic categories the words you've highlighted cover. For this ad, the following are the categories I came up with:

A.   **Attention to Detail**

B.   **Basic Computer and/or Technology Skills**

C.   **Budgeting**

D.   **Communication Skills (both giving and receiving)**

E.   **Customer service**

F.   **Organization and Planning**

G.   **Problem Solving**

H.   **Supervision Skills and Experience**

I.   **Teamwork**

Some of the qualifications and abilities may cover more than one category. For example 3c, "Establish positive and professional relationships," relates to both E – Customer Service and I – Teamwork.

Step 5: Make sure you meet any specific requirements. For example, you'd need to know First Aid and CPR for this position.

Step 6: Check for any Supplemental Questions at the end of the ad or on the application website.

Here is the ad I analyzed and marked with the categories I designated. The bold letters in parenthesis, for example **(A)**, **(B)**, **(C)** etc.), represent those categories listed above. They were not part of the original ad.

Child Care Program Assistant

Description

To perform a variety of duties related to assisting with planning, coordinating and supervising Child Care and/or preschool programs.

1)   EXAMPLES OF ESSENTIAL DUTIES – Duties may include, but are not limited to, the following:

a)   Maintain positive student relations **(E)** and follow disciplinary procedures.

b)   Notify **(D)** appropriate staff of any problems with regard to site maintenance, children or parents, and make recommendations as necessary.

c)   Help to maintain records and reports **(A)** as required; track and complete subsidized child care paperwork.

d)   Prepare reports **(A)**, schedules, and other administrative material.

e)   Coordinate supply needs.

f)   Monitor and adhere to the program budget **(C)**.

g)   Aid in training **(H)** of seasonal employees and volunteers.

h)   Mentor and direct **(H)** staff in all aspects of classroom management, curriculum and team building.

i)   Supervise **(H)** assigned temporary staff; schedule, train and monitor staff relative to assigned duties; review timekeeping system of assigned staff for accuracy.

j)   Build and maintain positive working relationships **(I)** with co-workers, other City employees, and the public using principles of good customer service.

k)   Perform related duties as assigned.

MINIMUM QUALIFICATIONS

2)   Knowledge of:

a)   Basic knowledge of modern methods, techniques, principles and procedures used in the planning and supervision of child care and/or preschool programs and facilities.

b)   Practices and methods of public relations and customer service **(E)**; techniques and principles of effective interpersonal communication **(D)**.

c)   Basic methodology of organizing groups, programs, and services in a recreational setting.

d)   Principles and techniques of first aid and CPR.

e)   Modern office equipment, methods, procedures, and computer hardware and software.

3)   Ability to:

a)   On a continuous basis, know and understand operations and observe safety rules; supervise children; stand for long periods of time; interpret, understand and follow policies and procedures, and explain operations and problem solve issues for the public and with staff.

b)   Intermittently set up booths, hang banners, move tables, chairs and carry supplies; participate with children on field trips, perform exercises with children; lift or carry weight of 45 pounds or less.

c)   Supervise children on playground.

d)   Establish positive and professional relationships **(E and I)** with children, co-workers and parents.

e)   Establish and maintain effective working relationships **(I)** with those contacted in the course of work.

f)   Make sound decisions with solid problem-solving **(G)** methods.

g)   Operate a computer as necessary to perform job duties.

h)   Understand and carry out written and oral directions.

i)   Maintain accurate and up–to–date records.

j)   Communicate **(D)** tactfully with customers.

k)   Communicate **(D)**effectively and concisely, both orally and in writing.

4)   Experience:

a)   Minimum of two (2) years of work experience in a licensed child care center or comparable group child care program, under the supervision of a person who would qualify as a teacher or director.

OR

b)   Two (2) seasons of paid experience in administering and coordinating recreation programs or a related field.

5)   Education and Training:

a)   Equivalent to completion of the twelfth (12th) grade, GED, or higher-level degree supplemented by completion of twelve (12) units in early childhood education, recreation, physical education, elementary education or related field.

6)   License or Certificate

a)   Possession of a valid California driver's license by date of appointment.

b)   Possession of CPR and First Aid certificates within six (6) months of hire.

SUPPLEMENTAL QUESTIONNAIRE

1. Have you completed twelve (12) college units in early childhood education, recreation, physical education or elementary education? Yes or No

1.5 How to Present Yourself

I'm putting this advice early in the book because it applies to many situations including networking and interviewing.

How you present yourself covers much more than how you dress. People form impressions of others in less than ten seconds. It's a blink of an eye. All of this advice is here to help you form an excellent impression.

Pay Attention to Your Body Language

People will notice your body language (consciously or unconsciously) before you ever open your mouth.

Make sure your arms aren't crossed and that your body language is open.

Smile and make eye contact. This is one of the most important things you can do in a social situation to make a good impression.

People cannot tell if you're shy. If you simply present yourself as a confident person, people will think you are a confident person. Smile, make eye contact and speak well and people will assume you're confident.

How to Make Eye Contact If You're Shy

I realize that for some people, making eye contact can be difficult.

There's an easy trick you can use if you fall into this category.

Simply look at the forehead or nose of the person you're talking to. It will appear to them as if you're looking them in the eye, but you don't have to hold their gaze. Make sure to practice this at home before you try it in the real world. I find myself focusing so much on trying to stare specifically at their nose that it's actually a little too intense.

The Handshake

Note: I would not recommend shaking hands during a global pandemic.

However, I'm keeping this section in the book in case you need the information at some future date.

If you are going to shake hands, you should try to achieve the Goldilocks handshake. It shouldn't be to firm or too soft. You want to go for something that's just right.

If you aren't sure about your handshake, practice with a friend that can give you feedback.

You may want to wash your hands with hot or warm water before you meet people professionally. There's research demonstrating that people trust individuals with warm hands. Warm hands are good. Additionally, washing your hands will get rid of sweaty palms, at least for a little while.

Don't touch your face if you've shaken hands with anyone. Wash or sanitize your hands as soon as possible.

Good Posture Is Key

I'm going to repeat something your parents probably told you to do multiple times: stand up straight.

Keep your shoulders back and straighten your spine.

A good way to practice this if you don't already display good posture is every time you go through a doorway, reset your posture so that you're standing up straight. If you do this all of the time, it should become habitual.

Go for That Mona Lisa Smile

When we're relaxed many of us will display a face that seems to be unfriendly, grumpy, or even angry; even when we don't feel those emotions. It's simply how your face looks when you fully relax. This characteristic is commonly referred to as resting bitch face. In this book I'm going to refer to it as Resting Angry Face (RAF).

During an interview and with any other interactions with potential employers, it is critical that you display a friendly face.

You don't need to fully smile, but you do need to avoid RAF.

You're going to want to replace RAF with a Mona Lisa smile.

Remember her smile in the paintings? It looks like she's smiling just a little bit. This is the look you should go for and here's an easy way to train yourself to avoid RAF.

Try this in front of a mirror so you can see how your face looks.

Start with a full smile with your lips closed.

Gradually relax your face until you're completely relaxed.

When your face is completely relaxed, if your lips tilt downward you may seem to have a grumpy face.

Now smile again and stop your lips in the last position before you completely relax. Your lips should be tilted slightly upwards. You'll notice that it's not a full smile but it should seem to be a little friendlier.

This is something you need to figure out and practice well ahead of your interview so that it becomes automatic.

Grooming

Good grooming is one of the most important things to do for all of your professional interactions and particularly the interview. It indicates attention to detail and respect for others.

Your hair should be freshly washed and tamed.

Hands should be washed.

Wear deodorant.

No perfume or cologne.

Fingernails

Your fingernails should be clean and well–trimmed. I would recommend nails on the shorter side. Longer nails can be distracting. Remember, you're going for a neutral look during the for the interview.

If you color your nails, I'd suggest a lighter neutral color nail polish. I've interviewed people where dark fingernails were definitely a distraction because the person talked with their hands and I lost track of what they were saying because I was watching their hands rather than listening to the content of their speech.

1.6 How to Talk Small

Because small talk is a critical skill needed for multiple parts of your job hunt, I'll talk about it here, in the general advice section. I want to provide a few specifics about how to make small talk in a variety of situations; such as informational interviews, happy hours, and conferences.

This section provides a short "how to" guide to making small talk. You'll also find more information about small talk in other sections of this book.

Small Talk Resources

One of the best books I've read on making small talk is *How to Talk to Anyone: 92 Little Tricks for Big Success in Relationships* by Leil Lowdnes. I would highly recommend it to anyone who wishes to polish their conversational skills. Even those of us who are already pretty good at small talk would benefit from this excellent guide.

Here are a few tips from this book:

You only need to add about 50 words to your vocabulary to seem more intelligent

Avoid clichés

Use specific language for description, rather than euphemisms

Don't make jokes at the expense of others

If you exchange business cards, write a note on the back with the date and location and something memorable about the meeting

You'll have to buy the book to get the other 87 tips.

Of course, there are also a plethora of resources online that will provide guidance on how to make small talk. "Small talk," "ice breakers," and "conversation starters" are good search terms for this type of information.

Practical Tips

Here are a few more things to keep in mind about making small talk and a good impression.

Keep it positive. Don't discuss things you don't like or that annoy you.

Easy questions that will help you discover topics you may have in common:

• What are they reading or watching?
• What do they do in their spare time?
• What are their hobbies?
• Where are they from?
• Where do they like to eat?
• What do they like to eat?
• Weather and sports are generally pretty safe and easy topics

It will be easier to move the conversation along if you are actually interested in the topic, so try to choose a topic that you would like to talk about. For example, if you don't like sports, choose a different topic for small talk.

Share something about yourself that relates to the topic that you've been discussing.

Listen to the responses and either agree with what they say or add to it.

Ask more questions or continue on the same theme.

Small Talk Example

In case you need an example of what this might sound like, here's an example:

Person 1 – Have you read any good books lately?

Person 2 – I know I'm a bit behind, but I've just finished The Hunger Games. It was really good.

Person 1 – It was really good. I loved the heroine Katniss Everdeen. What a great character. Have you seen the movies?

Person 2 – Yes, I have....

This is very similar to the rules of improv. "Yes And". You'll notice that Person 1 asked a question and then added something to the topic. You should attempt to agree with the person and then add something on the same topic.

If you aren't comfortable doing this, force yourself to practice whenever you're out in the world. An easy way is to start with situations that have low stakes such as chatting with people in the checkout counter.

Put away your phone and pay attention to the person or people you are with. Actively listen to them (i.e. don't do that thing we all do where we're just waiting for the other person to stop talking so that we can talk).

If it's an appropriate setting, and the small talk has gone well, ask for a business card and/or if they're on linked in. If so – can you connect to them? You'll be building your network. You never know when that connection may come in handy.

Chapter 2 – Networking

2.1 What Is Networking and Why Should I Care?

"If someone out of work knows only three words about their job hunt, those three words will be: resumes, interviews and networking."[2]

People already know the importance of resumes and interviewing. They aren't as likely to know how important networking is.

The importance of networking seems to be the thing that most people misunderstand about a job hunt.

I often hear people talking about applying on multiple job sites, getting their resume up to date. But I rarely hear people talk about networking.

It's been my experience that networking is the least understood, and yet one of the most important parts, of the job hunt.

Networking will greatly increase your chances of getting a job.

For example, 39.9% of hires are made through employee referral programs.[3]

People often ask what my most important job-hunting tip is and my response is always networking.

Many people who don't understand networking seem to think that in order to professionally network, you need to schmooze with other people like a used car salesman.

It's much simpler than that. You are simply introducing yourself to people, let everyone know that you're looking for a job and finding a way to systematically stay in touch, such as through LinkedIn.

Additionally, networking is essential in moving forward in your career once you get the job.

In this section, we'll cover the reasons why it's important such as:

• Options for networking
• Networking at conferences
• Business cards for networking
• Informational interviewing

When I chat with people about getting a job, they often ask for advice about how to improve their chances. The advice that I give most frequently is that they need to network. It's my top advice for any job seeker.

This often makes them uncomfortable because they don't understand what networking is. They see it as a sort of schmoozing and/or slimy activity conducted by used car salesman types. They think that only extroverts will excel at networking.

But networking is much simpler than that. You are simply introducing yourself to people and talking to them in order to form connections to others. You can also check in with people who are already in your network. Anyone can develop excellent networking skills.

You are putting yourself out into the world and connecting to others.

Why Is Networking Important?

There a multiple reasons why networking is important. Let's take a look at a few of the reasons why.

The Hidden Job Market

What is the hidden job market? It is the set of jobs that are never posted online. People recruit and hire employees through other means such as networking or employee referral programs.

I've seen a variety of statistics on the hidden job market. Most of them place it as at least 70–80% of all jobs.[4] There's even one survey that indicates 85% of all jobs are filled by networking.[5] That's a huge chunk of the market. "The Number one-way people discover a new job is through a referral."[6]

How do you access the hidden job market? Networking.

Inside Information

Beyond the hidden market, even if a job is posted on a board, your chances of getting the job greatly increase if you are connected in some way to an employee at a company or organization.

People who work for an organization can give you all sorts of inside information that can help you get the job. They can tell you about important trends. They can tell you if it's a decent place to work. They went through the hiring process so they obviously know what it's like. They may even remember something about the interview questions that were asked.

Networking is also important when you're trying to get information about an organization when you're applying for a job. If you know someone in the organization you can find out more about what they're really looking for, whether there's an inside candidate, as well as information about the culture of the organization. and the technology they use. All of this is extremely important when you're going to interview for a job and will give you a leg up.

Career Exploration

It's a way to explore careers. One of the best ways to get a sense of a job is to talk to someone about the day–to–day requirements of a job. It will also give you a sense of where you'd best fit in your career. For example, in the library world there are multiple types of libraries. Academic, public, special, school, government. They're all quite different. If you set up an informational interview with a librarian or library worker, you'll get a better sense of which type of library will work best for you.

More Contacts = Higher Odds of Getting a Job

The simplest reason you should network is that the more people you know, the more connections you have to potential employment. For example, if you let people know that you're looking for a job, they may send you information about job opportunities or other relevant information such as career fairs. People will send you information about opportunities and jobs.

You Don't Know Who People Know

Most people have connections to other circles and this can be useful to you. For example, it's fairly obvious that I have quite a few library connections. However, I also know quite a few people in environmental regulations simply because I have friends in that field. It's not something that you'd know if you chatted with me casually, but if you mentioned that you were looking for a job in that field, I would probably offer to connect you to one of the people I know in that field.

You don't know who people know. You'd be surprised at connections. Each person you meet may know someone who would be a valuable contact.

For example, I was at a conference one time, chatting with another attendee who I had just met. It turned out that her significant other was an assistant professor in an anthropology department at a local university. When I returned to work after the conference, I was working with another student who was interested in the field of anthropology. I was able to connect the 2nd student with the professor. They started an email correspondence that was a great source of information for the student about the field and a professional connection the field they wished to enter. The key is to pay attention when you realize that someone may know someone who would be of value to you and don't be afraid to ask for contact information. And make sure to let your friends know that you're looking for a job or information and they may be able to help you network and connect to others.

People Are More Likely to Hire Known Quantities

This may be somewhat obvious but it's still worth stating. People are more likely to trust a known quantity or at least give them the benefit of the doubt. Networking can be particularly important if you fall outside of traditional expectations.

For example, if you're an older worker hiring managers may not expect you to have good technology skills because a common perception of older workers is that they have lesser technology skills or are even afraid of it. However, if someone in an organization knows you personally, you can break this expectation.

You Don't Fit the Mold

Networking is the most important for candidates who don't fit the model profile for what the organization is searching for such as older workers or people with disabilities.

It's also extra important when the job market is tight.

Now let's talk about networking opportunities you can use.

If You Are Unemployed

There's often a feeling of shame when you lose a job, regardless of the reasons. This is completely understandable and it makes it likely that you may want to hide this fact from the world.

However, if you lose your job, it's critical that you let everyone you know that you're looking for work. Given everything that I've discussed in this section, particularly given that you don't know who people know, your job hunt will be much more effective if you take this step. People will understand and offer support.

Book Recommendations

All three of these are excellent for learning how to network:

- *How to Talk to Anyone: 92 Little Tricks for Big Success in Relationships* by Leil Lowdnes

- *Networking for People Who Hate Networking: A Field Guide for Introverts, the Overwhelmed, and the Underconnected* by Devorah Zack

- *Work the Pond* by Darcy Rezac

2.2 LinkedIn

If you are looking for a job and only do one thing to improve your chances, you should sign up on LinkedIn. It is essential to any job hunt.

I always ask jobhunters if they are on LinkedIn? It's not optional if you're looking for a job.

As the 2014 edition of *What Color is Your Parachute* states, "Be sure to get on it [LinkedIn]."

Social professional networks are the #1 source of quality hires.[7]

Given that LinkedIn is the top professional social network, LinkedIn is the best option for professional networking when you're looking for a job.

Using social media may increase your chances of finding a finding a job. However, even if you don't use any other social media sites, LinkedIn is the one website you should join in order to utilize social media in your job search. It is the largest and most popular professional website. I'm devoting this entire section to LinkedIn because of the importance of this site, both while you are looking for a job and also as your career progresses once you have been hired.

I will cover a few basics here, but if you'd like to become a power user of LinkedIn, there are many books and websites you can consult. I'd recommend The Power Formula for LinkedIn Success: Kick-start Your Business, Brand, and Job Search by Wayne Breitbarth. It's a nice introduction to some of the powerful options for this website.

What Is LinkedIn?

LinkedIn is the most important, largest networking site for professionals. It's the Facebook of the professional world. In terms of social media site, it has been around for a while, since 2003. Other professional networking sites may have similar features and services; however, LinkedIn is still the most important professional social media site because it is so large. As of 2020, LinkedIn has over 690 million users in over 200 countries.[8]

Why Join LinkedIn?

In case you need a few more reasons to convince you to join LinkedIn, here are a few you should consider.

Larger Pool

You'll have access to a much larger pool of people than you would in real life because of the size of this site and the ease it allows connecting to others. LinkedIn allows you to connect to and keep in track and touch with a much larger group of people than you would otherwise be able to. I am connected to over 400 people on LinkedIn. It would be much harder to maintain this network in another form. More people in your network means that you will have a larger and more varied network and a better chance to find a job.

It's Easier to Keep in Touch

People move positions. Email addresses change. Because people update their own information, once you're connected on LinkedIn you don't have to worry about updating your address book. As long as your contacts are connected to the site, you'll be able to contact them. LinkedIn makes it easier to keep track of your professional network.

Visibility and Portability

Your LinkedIn profile contains so much more information about your professional life than a resume will. It is also far more visible. You can make business cards with your LinkedIn URL and carry them with you.

LinkedIn also makes it easier to see who other people are connected to, which can be invaluable information. You can easily see if one of your connections knows anyone at a specific institution. They may even be able to provide you with an introduction through the website.

More Varied Network

You can connect to more people in more varied settings than you would normally be able to connect to in the "real world". LinkedIn allows you to connect to people in different fields because people are connected to a wider variety of other people via LinkedIn than they might be in real life. This means you have access to all sorts of different people outside of your field.

Great Source of Information

It's a great source of information you can use to improve your resume and other application materials.

You can look at other profiles to improve yours. You can use this information to improve your other application materials.

You can use it to research companies, people or potential employers. If you search for a company in people search you can find people who may be connected to that company.

Although it's particularly important when you're looking for a job, it's also a great resource once you've found that job.

Ask Questions

You can ask questions of your network. I've found this to be particularly useful for finding an expert on a particular topic.

Start Discussions

You can start discussions with Groups. There are a huge number of useful groups on LinkedIn that allow you to can start a discussion and ask advice from others without a direct connection. These groups give you access to a wider and deeper knowledge base than you would otherwise have access to. They can provide you with a variety of different types of support and advice from peers and experts. They would be particularly useful for anyone who doesn't have any peers at work to discuss issues and problems that may come up. If you want to explore groups, starting at the Interests link in the main menu to find groups that interest you.

Expand Your Network

You can also use groups to connect to new people on LinkedIn. If you make a personal connection to someone in a group send them an invitation to connect if you really interacted and connected on a personal level.

Research

You can use it to research companies, people or potential employers. If you search for a company in people search you can find people who may be connected to that company.

Recommendations

People can easily write you recommendations which are public on LinkedIn. You can also write recommendations for others and strengthen your connections. Recommendations are much more personal than endorsements and do carry weight for anyone viewing your profile, particularly recruiters.

Ask a Wider Circle

It's easier to contact a wider group of people at one time who you've known from a variety of networks. For example, I can email my whole LinkedIn network to ask questions about a variety of topics.

How to Set up Your Account

LinkedIn is similar to any other account you'll create online. You'll need a login and password. You'll need an email address that will connect to the site.

Decide which email address you'll use to connect to the website. It should be something that you check somewhat regularly so that you'll see any notifications and communications from the website. If you think you'll stay in your current position for some time and it doesn't go against any policies, you can certainly use your work email address. However, if you think that you may regularly change employers or you aren't comfortable linking your work email to this account, you can link it to an outside account. This is also true if you are holding down more than one job. If you are actively seeking employment, you should already have an email account you are using for all of your job hunting needs. Use that account to connect to LinkedIn.

Setting up Your Profile

You must set up a profile to use LinkedIn.

As with all other tools, particularly social media tools, you may or may not want to fill in your complete profile. LinkedIn will continually nudge you to add more information about yourself. If you are currently looking for a job you will want to provide as much information and add as much content as you can. However, if you are using LinkedIn for networking purposes, as I do, you may only want to fill in the sections that will help you connect to other people. Decide what works best for you and ignore the sections you don't want to fill in.

However, having said that, for all LinkedIn users, there are a few sections of your profile that you should fill in if you're going to use the website.

As with the rest of your job-hunting portfolio, spelling and grammar must be perfect. Make sure to have a friend or two review your profile, particularly if you are actively seeking employment.

You Can Use the Free Version

Although you can sign up for the Premium version, you don't need to pay for LinkedIn. You can access a huge number of features using the free version. I have never used the paid version, although I might in certain circumstances, if I were looking for a job for example.

Profile Photo

Your photo is the first thing anyone will see when they view your profile and it's extremely important. Go to the next section (2.3) to find out why it's so important, as well as tips, dos, and don'ts for any online portraits you use for job hunting.

What Are the Keywords?

Make sure you include the right keywords for your profile. If you aren't sure what these might be, look at the profiles of others and at job postings and position descriptions.

Professional Headline

This displays next to your profile photo. It sets the tone for your profile. You can either use your current job title, or tweak it a little bit for emphasis or to display a range of talents. For example, mine reads Library and Information Technology Program Coordinator, Librarian, Job Coach and Mentor at Sacramento City College which provides a little more information than my job title will by itself. Your professional headline can be particularly useful if you have a generic job title or a job title people don't understand. For example, what does Consultant mean?

Work History

At a minimum, you should fill in your work history with your job titles, organizations, locations and the dates of your work history. This is the information that will allow you to connect with others on LinkedIn. Once you've filled in the basic information about your work history, you can add a wide variety of other information such as duties, media, presentations, photographs and much more.

Education

Education is another section that will allow you to connect to others on the website which means you should fill it in. If you add the colleges and universities you have attended, you can connect with others from that institution. This can be one of your richest networking opportunities and can also provide you with a way to connect to that long–lost classmate. You don't have to have graduated from an institution to add it to your profile. If you are a new student at a college, add it as soon as you're enrolled and connect to your classmates and professors as you earn your degree.

Skills and Endorsements

This section of your profile can be a little strange because people may endorse you for skills that you don't think you actually have. However, you can control this section and add skills you'd like people to endorse you for and rearrange the order in which your skills appear. You can also delete skills where you have no expertise. People do not generally give a lot of weight to this section because we all know that it's a little too easy to endorse others in your network without knowing about your skills. However, I believe that it can still add to your profile and the impression you give if you have a lot of endorsements in an area, particularly if it's specific enough and if you've worked on keeping this section accurate. If 50 people say you're have a particular skill, that can have some weight, even if it's on a subconscious level.

Your LinkedIn URL (Uniform Resource Locator)

Make sure to edit your public profile URL. You can add this to any promotional materials such as your resume and business cards.

The Rest of Your Profile

Once you've done the minimum with your profile and filled in your photo, headline, work history, education and edited your skills you can add as much other information as you'd like. You can also add more photographs and content to really personalize your profile. If you already have a resume or CV it's easy to copy and paste that information into your profile. The more information you include, the fuller your profile will be which can improve your odds of finding a job.

Etiquette to Connecting to Others on LinkedIn

On the whole you should keep it real and connect to people you know. It is generally considered to be bad form to try to connect to people you don't actually know using LinkedIn. Unless you have a job that requires you to connect to a lot of people you may not know that well, most of your connections should be to people you have met.

I will occasionally add people to my network who are strangers if they are employed by a legitimate organization that is part of my industry. However, I rarely connect with people I haven't personally met without an introduction of some sort. The site is powerful because it reflects actual connections that people have to each other in real life. If you connect to a lot of people you don't really know, it dilutes the power of your profile. It's pretty obvious when you've simply collected a bunch of connections on LinkedIn. This can make quite a bad impression and hurt your chances of getting a job.

When you send a connection request, try to personalize it, particularly if the connection request is to someone who you don't know that well. Change the language of the automatic message that is generated. A personal touch can make a difference in the impression you make.

Friends of Friends

One exception to this rule is that LinkedIn allows you to make introductions between people in your network. Connecting with an introduction is different just as introducing yourself to a total stranger is different than being introduced by someone you have in common. "LinkedIn is, far and away, the most advantageous social networking tool available to job seekers and business professionals today. Far and away."[9]

2.3 Your Online Portrait

With an online presence such as your LinkedIn profile, you are branding yourself and your online portrait is the most identifiable part of your brand.

Much of your job hunt should be tied into your online presence, particularly on social media. By at least one estimate 92% of employers are recruiting through social media, particularly LinkedIn.[10] In order to be successful in this online realm, you need to use a professional image in order to represent yourself. This is critical for job hunting. For example, "According to LinkedIn, a profile with a photo gets up to 14 times more profile views."[11] In fact, recruiters spend 19% of their time looking at your profile photo.[12] Given that they may only spend six seconds reviewing your profile or resume, the profile photo is extremely important.[13]

Choose One Image for Your Brand

You need to choose a specific image to represent yourself online professionally. In other areas of your life, such as your personal Facebook page, it doesn't particularly matter if you choose one specific image.

You can be far more creative. However, wherever you're representing yourself professionally online, you should use the same image, a portrait photograph.

Have Someone Take a Photo of You

You do not have to pay someone to take a professional head shot to use as your online portrait. However, you should take a little extra effort with your profile photograph. Rather than simply posting an existing photo that may not quite be appropriate, or that you've cropped to show your head, actually get someone to take a new photo of you that you can use professionally.

There are a couple of benefits of doing this. Taking the time to get a good photograph falls into the category of going the extra mile. You didn't simply find a vacation shot from your computer to post. You went to a little extra trouble to dress up and take the photo. Even if this isn't apparent on a conscious level, it should register on some level that you went the extra mile. The photograph will also be appropriate for this setting (i.e. facial portrait, good lighting, appropriately dressed) rather than something that isn't quite right.

Find a Friend

My best advice is, unless you have a friend who's a professional photographer and can take a really good shot, simply go outside and have a friend or loved one take a nice photograph in front of a neutral background such as a wall or plants. If you have a friend or loved one take the photo you are more likely to be relaxed and this should produce a better photograph.

Photography Specifics

Elongate your neck and push your chin forward a bit.

Be careful about wearing patterns close to your face, they may be distracting in photographs.

Natural Light Is Best

Take the photograph in natural light, i.e. outside. But not in direct sunlight which would be too harsh. Try to think of something funny, your smile will be more natural. There is a lot more advice you'll find online if you search for ways to take a good picture.

Can You See Your Face?

Make sure you can really see your face in the photograph? Choose a photo from the waist up.

Don't use any photographs where you're far away such as long shots. Your face should be the most prominent part of the photo. Don't use any photos with more than one person in the photograph. Which one is you?

Dress Professionally

Put on a professional outfit. Although this should be a portrait from the waist up, wear an entire outfit. You'll feel more professional and this will be reflected in the photograph. Select neutral clothes, jewelry and makeup.

Is It Recent?

The portrait should be fairly recent. Don't choose anything that looks too out of date.

Does It Look Like You?

The photograph should actually resemble what you look like in person. What would happen if an employer were to view your profile and it didn't match what you actually look like? If they met you and couldn't recognize you? What impression would that leave them? You never know who you might meet in person.

A Good Example

Here is an example of a photograph that would work really well for professional networking and online profiles such as LinkedIn.

It was taken by my daughter on my iPhone, using portrait mode in my backyard.

The lighting is good – I took it outside in the evening, which is a good time to take photos. The light will be bright, but not direct which would cause a lot of shadows.

It's a headshot and you can see my face and smile clearly.

The background is neutral.

I'm wearing professional clothing but it's not particularly formal.

I look relaxed and happy.

These are all criteria that you should strive for with your online photo profile.

It doesn't have to be a professional head shot, just a good photo. Take a minute and have a friend take a good photo you can use for your online presence. Don't just use an existing photo.

You should be smiling, happy and relaxed. You should be dressed and groomed professionally. Refer to section 4.2 for more information about how to dress professionally.

You will be more likely to be relaxed and smiling if someone you like takes the photo. It's particularly effective if they get you to laugh so that you have a natural smile.

Do You Have a Common Name?

It particularly important to have an online portrait if you have a common name and you want people to be able to connect to you online. My name is fairly unusual. There are not that many other women named Pamela Posz. Since people I meet usually know I'm a librarian, I'm very easy to find. However, if my name was Jennifer Smith, it would be even more important for me to post a photo with my profile. I would need a good identifiable photo if I wanted people to find me rather than one of the other Jennifer Smiths. I would also try to display a photo that was somewhat unique, perhaps with a background that indicated something about what I'd like to convey.

Don'ts

If you take a photo specifically for your professional profile photo, you will need to avoid these pitfalls.

But I wanted to mention them specifically just in case.

No Dating Profile Photos

If you've submitted a photo to a dating website or app this is probably not the photo you want to post in your LinkedIn profile. What makes you attractive to dates is not the same as what makes you attractive to employers, although there may be some crossover. You're better safe than sorry with this one.

No Selfies

If it is at all possible, try to get someone else to take your photo or use a tripod of some sort. Selfies aren't your best option. Even with a selfie–stick, the angle and facial expressions on selfies often create weird photos and they are usually identifiable as a selfie. This is bad because it indicates low effort rather than taking your time.

It's really important to avoid selfies taken in a restroom or toilet, or even photos with any sort of backgrounds that look like you took them in a bathroom stall.

This is not the Time for the "Fun" Photos

Definitely do not use any photos that involve drinking alcohol or partying of any sort.

Do not use your vacation photographs. A beach scene doesn't really say "I'm ready to work."

Naked Photos Live Forever

This section falls into the common sense isn't always common category.

If you already know that you should never post or send naked or inappropriate photos of yourself on any sort of computer network (i.e. the Internet), skip this section.

For those of you who aren't aware, this is a reminder that anything you post online is no longer yours and may be shared with the world. It can easily live forever, even if you have deleted it from your account. Screen shots anyone? The cloud? Even more worrisome, it can be altered once you send it out or post it. Once you press enter and send it out on the Internet, you are no longer in control of that information. The content no longer belongs to you.

There are many examples of people losing opportunities or jobs because of posts, tweets, photos or videos that they thought were never going to follow them, particularly because they assumed that they were posting anonymously or had posted the information a long time ago. You should not post anything online that you wouldn't be willing to see on a billboard by the freeway or on the front page of the New York Times.

You should assume that employers will Google you and look at Twitter and Facebook. I heard a specific example that illustrates the "no naked photos rule" from a friend who was screening applications for an open position at their company. Part of the screening process involved looking at social media accounts of all of the applicants. One had posted artistic naked photos on their Facebook profile. The photos were tasteful and obviously taken by a professional for a retail catalog, but the applicant still did not get the job.

No naked photos ever!

Check Your Settings

This is a more general warning, be very careful about the privacy settings on your phone, particularly in terms of loading photos into the cloud. Once something is in the cloud, it could easily turn up online where you least expect it. Watch those privacy settings for any photos you wish to remain private.

2.4 Internships and Volunteering

Internships and volunteer work both offer advantages to those who are looking for a job, particularly if you are trying to enter a new field. They can provide on the job experience and training, which is extremely valuable to employers and is an excellent addition to any resume. However, volunteer work and internships are not identical experiences.

Volunteer work generally consists of working for an organization without pay. Sometimes this is formalized, sometimes not. An internship is generally a formalized relationship where one person works for another or for an organization. The work may be paid or unpaid. Additionally, internships are often tied to educational experiences. For example, a degree may require an internship in order to graduate.

Internships are special and magical opportunities that are viewed at a much higher level than volunteer experiences.

People often assume that if you offer free labor, an organization or employer will be happy to have you work. This may not be true for a variety of reasons. Preparing anyone for a work environment takes a fair amount of time and energy. For example, the worker must be trained and supervised. The employer may wish to provide feedback. The worker must be added to the work schedule. Volunteers may also disappear without notice and can be unreliable. If you simply show up to volunteer, you be turned away because there's a fair amount of work in training and supervising volunteers.

Internships are generally considered to be more valuable than volunteering because they are measurable and involve a formalized relationship with an official organization such as a college or university. They have a much higher level of accountability and there are consequences if any problems come up. If you show up as part of an internship, it is far more likely that you will get your foot in the door, than you would if you simply showed up as a volunteer.

Internships tend to provide a much higher level of work experience than volunteering. Volunteer work is more likely to be basic and it may take some time before you are entrusted with higher level responsibilities.

Although both internships and volunteer work can provide good experiences and should be included on your resume, internships should be prioritized.

Make Sure to Complete an Internship Before You Graduate

Often the only way to obtain an internship is via a college or university. Schools and employers usually have official internships agreements. You should maximize any internship opportunities that are available to you as a student. If you are in college, you should make sure that you have completed at least one internship before you graduate.

This is even more critical if the program which you are attending is offered completely online. Employers want to make sure that you are employable. If you've only gone through a program that is completely online, there may be concerns about your social skills or other issues.

Once you graduate, internship opportunities will not be the same. You will not have access to the same internship opportunities that you had as a student.

The one exception to this is that if you've already been working in an internship for a while, even if you graduate you may be able to continue volunteering with that employer because they already know you and you are already vetted.

If you have an opportunity to complete more than one internship and it works with your life, you should do so. This will expand your resume, your professional network and give you a different set of on the job training and experiences. It's a second set of contacts for your professional network.

Finding Internships

The best way to find internships is through educational institutions such as colleges and universities. They often have internship offices that will assist with placement. Figure out early in your academic career how internships work on campus so that you avoid missing deadlines and other issues that may arise.

If you have already graduated see if you can find an internship class that will allow you to complete an internship. This can be an effective strategy if you've been out of the workforce for a while. Community Colleges may be one of your best options for this.

Application Process

The application process for volunteering may be formal or informal. The organization may have a process set up for those who wish to volunteer, or a volunteer might simply show up at a location and work.

The application process for an internship has usually been formalized. The applicant would submit an application and go through a short interview process. The applicant should be prepared to submit a cover letter and resume and there will probably be an interview of some sort.

Time Frame

There is generally a time frame on an internship such as a semester, six months or a year. Because volunteer opportunities are often less formalized, they may be a onetime or ongoing.

How to Be a Good Intern

Demonstrate good employee behavior, i.e. don't be late, don't flake out, behave professionally, good communication skills.

You are there to learn, not to tell anyone how they can improve things.

Ask permission for areas in which you haven't been trained or before trying to make any changes.

Act as if the internship is a job. On the first day you should show up early or at least on time and have taken care of any critical details such as parking arrangements. Not being able to find parking will not be accepted as a valid excuse for why you are 30 minutes late.

Come prepared with something on which you can take notes. A pad of paper is probably your best option. There is less chance for distraction and if you use an electronic device such as your phone, your trainer may wonder if you're doing activities not related to the internship, such as checking Facebook.

Dress appropriately/professionally. If you aren't sure about what this means, you should ask your internship supervisor before you begin. Pay attention to how the employees dress and model your wardrobe on that.

Don't be afraid to say "I don't know" and ask questions. It always makes me nervous when I'm training someone and they don't have any questions. There's no way that they could absorb and understand everything that I say. Which means that at some later point it's likely that they'll do something wrong.

Make sure you get input from your internship supervisor. If you don't receive this, make sure to pursue it. You are actually there to learn.

If the employer likes you, they may find a way to hire you or will at least help you find a job somewhere else.

Before you leave the internship, ask for a letter of recommendation. I discuss the etiquette and process for doing this in section 3.9.

If something unexpected comes up in your personal life and you have to leave the internship or volunteer opportunity sooner than planned, make sure to communicate with your supervisor and give notice if possible. Don't leave them in the lurch. Always leave with a good impression.

2.5 Networking Opportunities

Now that we've talked about why it's important to network, let's go through a few specifics about how to network.

Professionally your goal should be to establish, expand (meet new people), and maintain your network.

You will need a way to contact and stay in touch with those in your network. I've already extensively discussed LinkedIn in section 2.2 because LinkedIn is my favorite networking tool. It's the preeminent professional online networking platform. It simplifies and streamlines keeping in touch with people in my professional network and it will help you expand your network because it also allows you to easily connect to individuals who are contacts of the people in your network. For example, as of 2018 I have 544 people in my network. If I were to connect to just 8 additional people who are contacts of my network, that would total over 4400 connections. The math is very much in your favor with LinkedIn.

Network Your Way Into a Job

I believe networking is one of the keys to being successful in many aspects of your life. For example, when I was a new parent, forming a network of other moms definitely kept me sane.

But when you're looking for a job, networking is one of the best ways to increase your odds of getting the job you want.

What Do You Have to Offer?

Networking goes in more than one direction and involves both give and take. Although I've said it will increase your chances of getting a job, you will not do well if people just feel that you're connecting to them so that they can get you a job. The goal with networking should be to form connections that can be beneficial to everyone involved. Think about what you can offer to the other person rather than just what they can do for you.

Small Pond

Networking is a great way to improve your chances of getting a job, but make sure you make a good impression while you're doing it. Cities and towns are often pretty small ponds when it comes to different groups and professions. You do not know who others know and there may be unexpected connections between people that you aren't aware of. Or there may be one person you encounter who really knows everyone. Don't make a bad impression. It could kill your chances of getting hired.

Prepare Your Networking Tools

Update your LinkedIn profile and make sure it includes a good photo (see section 2.3).

There are some professions (for example graphic design, photography, web design) where you'll need a portfolio that people can find online, in addition to your LinkedIn profile.

Set up the LinkedIn app on your phone. This makes it easy to connect at networking events.

Make business cards that have the URL for your LinkedIn profile (section 2.2).

You should also update your resume and any other relevant application materials.

Ready, Set, Network!

Start by letting your current network know that you're looking for a job.

Your current network includes the following:

- Family
- Friends
- Coworkers (if you're not worried that your employer knows you're looking for a job)
- Neighbors

- Acquaintances
- Former teachers and professors who you have had a good relationship with and have maintained contact with

In other words, everyone you know.

Okay, maybe not everyone. But you should let most of the people you know that you're actively looking for a job. You don't know where it may lead.

Places to Expand Your Network

Now that you've let your current network know that you're looking for a job, you should start to increase your network by meeting and connecting to new people. Here are a few networking options you might want to try.

Your Alma Mater

If you have attended college, there are a number of ways your college connections can be useful in expanding your network and making connections.

Colleges and universities frequently set up specific networking opportunities for alumni and current students because they realize that networking can be one of the biggest benefits for attending a college. People don't pay huge sums of money to attend Harvard or Stanford just because they offer excellent academics. One of the main reasons, other than the academics, is the networks that these colleges provide to their graduates.

If you are currently attending a college, I'd start by contacting the career center to see what networking opportunities (such as career fairs) are available.

If you have graduated, start with the alumni center.

If you're at a networking event and you meet someone with a connection to your school, it's a great topic of conversation and an immediate connection. This is true whether they attended a while ago or if they are currently attending the college.

Here are a few specific examples of questions you can ask to get the conversation going:

• What were your favorite places on and off campus?
• What did you major in?
• What did you enjoy about your experience at this school?
If it doesn't seem like it will offend ask "When did you attend?" Just be a little careful with this question. You may not want to bring this up if it seems like it's been a while since they attended.

Professional Happy Hours

I am a firm believer in the power of the happy hour. They are one of my favorite networking opportunities. They allow you to connect to others with similar interests in a more relaxed and less structured setting. They don't require a lot of preparation or a large time commitment. They're usually not too expensive. They're a great way to connect to others.

There are all sorts of Happy Hours that offer the ability to professionally connect to others. You can Google "professional happy hour" to see what's out there. These are a little more specific than generic happy hours and will be attended by people who are interested in networking or connecting to others in their field.

There is a bit of etiquette though. Keep these ideas in mind when you're at a happy hour. If you aren't much of a drinker don't worry. You don't have to drink alcohol to participate in the Happy Hour. However, on the other side, remember not to imbibe too heavily. If you do become intoxicated, this can make a bad impression. Even though Happy Hours are less formal, they are still professional and if you make a bad impression because you're drunk this may follow you and affect your ability to get a job.

2.6 Professional Organizations

One of your best opportunities for networking can be found through professional organizations.

What are professional organizations?

Professional organizations, as one might expect from the name, are organizations based around a specific profession. For example, the American Library Association is the giant umbrella organization for all types of libraries in the United States.

Additionally, there are usually a variety of more specific organizations that have been established for different professions. For example, the Public Library Association, Special Libraries Association, and Medical Libraries Association are all examples of professional organizations that have been formed for specific subsets of the library profession.

Geography is another way of subdividing professional organizations. For example, in the United States regional (such as the northeast, northwest, western, etc.), state level, local geographic regions such as the bay area in California, and even more specifically such as city or county chapters are all geographic subdivisions for organizations.

There are other ways to specifically subdivide professional organizations, but geography and subject specialization are two of the main options.

For job hunting purposes, search for professional organizations related to your field and look for options at the national and local level.

Why Join?

- Professional Organizations offer a number of invaluable services including:
- Job hunting support services such as job boards and places to post your resume.
- Conferences (these offer amazing networking opportunities) (section 2.7)
- Scholarship opportunities
- Networking opportunities

Find Your Local Chapter

I strongly urge you to join the local chapter of your professional organization, particularly if it's an active chapter, i.e. it hosts a lot of activities.

Local events provide one of the best networking opportunities, allowing members to meet other professionals in the same field, in the same geographic area. This proximity makes it easier to connect and stay in touch with each other.

The most direct way to form strong professional connections with others in your area is to join the governing board of the organization. As a board member you'll gain valuable experience, particularly in event planning and hosting. Serving as a board member is also an excellent way to build your professional resume. Volunteering for the organization offers a lower level way to serve the organization and build your resume, without having to commit the same amount of time that you would as a board member.

Save Money

The cost of joining professional organizations may seem to be prohibitively expensive. However, there are a few ways to save money, which may make it more likely that you'll join one.

If possible, join the organization when you're a student. The student rates are much, much, much cheaper. For example, the student rate might be $30 while the professional rate is $300.

If you're not going to attend the main annual conference of the organization, see if you can simply join the local chapter rather than the national one if that option is available.

If you are going to attend the annual conference, it's usually worth joining the organization for that year. The conference registration will be cheaper and you'll have access to all of the services that the organization offers for that year.

Even if you aren't a member, you can usually attend events hosted by the organization, most importantly, the conferences.

Even with the expense, joining organizations, is generally worth the cost, given how much they can move your career along by connecting you to people within your field. This is particularly true if you are job hunting.

2.7 Conferences, Conferences, Conferences

One of the best things about professional organizations is that they host conferences.

Conferences serve a variety of purposes and can be an important part of any job hunt.

Many conferences actually serve as the annual meeting for a professional organization. Organizational governance activities (such as elections and committee meetings) may happen during the conference.

Conferences provide information about what is happening in a particular field. Attendees are there to gain knowledge and skills and to keep up with new trends. A good conference will provide an excellent opportunity to learn about different topics, particularly new and emerging areas in a field or area of study.

People attend conferences in order to present information. For some fields, such as academia, presenting at conferences is an essential part of advancing your career. The number, level, and quality of presentations may be one of the main ways in which you are evaluated for promotion.

Conferences also provide a way to make an in-person connection to vendors and check out all of the new products in a field.

If there's a conference that interests you, but you cannot afford it (many conferences are fairly expensive), look for scholarships. These will often defray or cover the cost in part or in total. If the conference is local, look for volunteer opportunities. Sometimes if you volunteer at a conference, you can attend a few of the activities, check out the exhibits, or at least attend some of the social activities such as happy hours.

If you are truly unable to attend a conference because of cost, distance, or another factor, you can still follow the conference on social media sites such as Twitter or Instagram. You just need to know the #hashtag. You can also review the conference proceedings after it's over which is an invaluable glimpse into the cutting edge of what is happening in a profession. This can be extremely valuable information when you're interviewing. Studying recent conference proceedings will allow you to see the most up to date information about what is happening in a specific profession. It's a way to prepare for interview questions about the latest and greatest.

You can look for jobs at a conference, there's usually a career expo where employers interview and hire during the conference. If you are attending a conference in order to find a new position, you should follow much of the advice from this book. Dress professionally. Carry multiple resumes and cover letters. Carry a copy of your full work history for information that isn't included on your resume. Make sure that your references are up to date and aware that you're interviewing during the conference. Do a little research on the organization to which you're applying. There's often a conference job board where you can upload your resume and/or work history that will be accessible to employers during the conference so they can find you and potentially interview you.

It's the Networking

I occasionally get the question, why aren't all conferences virtual in the 21st century? Wouldn't it be less expensive? Can't you simply post the presentations online?

As a friend of mine joked about the Internet Librarian conference I was attending, "Why isn't it all online? Why are you meeting... [in person]?"

The answer is that it's the networking. There may be a few other factors, but mostly it's networking. Networking is one of the most valuable parts of attending a conference, and at this point, there's no equivalent way to make it happen in an online format (2nd life anyone?).

Networking is one of my favorite reasons to attend conferences. It offers one of the best opportunities to extend your network in ways you would not otherwise have access to. If the conference is national or international you can connect to others all over the country or world. It also offers access to people at more different levels (entry level, managers, presidents, etc.) than you would normally encounter. You might meet someone important who's willing to connect and/or chat.

Conferences are one of the best places to grow your professional network.

Whenever I attend a conference, I try to come home with at least 10–20 new contacts I can add to my network.

Conference Networking 101

So how to do you network at a conference?

At the conference you simply need to introduce yourself wherever you can to anyone you meet.

It's really that simple.

Here are a few specific networking strategies if you're not sure how to do it:

Look for fellow attendees outside of the official conference location. I've met many people while out to lunch or dinner in the vicinity of the conference. Attendees often forget to take off their badges when they leave the convention center and so it's really easy to spot them. If you find yourself next to a person who's obviously attending the conference, strike up a conversation.

Help others to network – introduce people you know to other people you know.

Look for conference newbies. There are often visual clues (such as conference ribbons) that indicate who the first timers are.

Look for groups of 2 people – it's easier to carry on a conversation with 2 than 1.

If you're attending with someone you know, make sure you don't simply socialize with that person.

Introduce yourself and talk to others as much as possible, particularly people you don't already know.

If you're attending with someone you know, make sure you don't spend all of your time with that person.

If you sit next to someone new, introduce yourself.

Help others network by connecting people from your network who may not already know each other who or who you've just met.

Look for networking events in the conference proceedings. They often occur in the evening and offer food and beverages (dinner!).

Easy Ice Breaking Questions at a Conference:

- Ask people where they're from.
- Ask them if they've attended any really good sessions.
- Ask them about their organization.

Name Tag on the Right Side

If you are right-handed you are likely to place the name tag on the left side because you put it on with your right hand. Instead, put it on your right side. This makes it easier for anyone shaking your hand to read your name. It's a little tweak but it can make it a little easier for others to remember your name.

Hang Out With People You Don't Know

Introduce yourself to new people, don't wait for others to introduce themselves to you.

If you are attending an event with people you already know, make sure to sit with and engage with other people whenever possible.

For example, if you are attending a lunch, make sure to sit next to people you don't already know.

Look for pairs of people to meet. It's a little less intimidating to approach 2 rather than a bigger group and a little easier to keep the conversation going with a group of at least two.

Get That Contact Information

Because you will be meeting a large number of people whenever you go to a conference, you will need to have a quick means to exchange information so that you can reconnect after the conference. If you are in a strongly technological field, I'd imagine that you simply connect with each other via the LinkedIn app, or something similar.

However, for many fields, business cards are the easiest way to quickly exchange personal information.

My first rule of conferences is to bring your business cards.

Although business cards may seem to be a little "old school" to some, they are a useful part of professional life and are particularly important for networking and attending conferences.

You're meeting all of these new people; you need to make it easy for them to find you.

Let's talk about how to do business cards.

Networking at Conferences

Conferences are a great place to network; in fact, they are one of the easiest places to network. If you haven't been to a conference before, you may think that the main point of conferences is to learn new things at the conference sessions. This is obviously one of the main reasons why you'd go.

However, the other major reason to attend is to network with other people in your profession.

There are many ways in which you can network, but conferences are particularly effective because an entire cross–section from an organization may attend. This means that you have a chance to interact with people you might not normally come into contact with, such as individuals in the higher levels of an organization.

Now let's look at how business cards can enable networking and are particularly important when you're going to attend a conference.

2.8 Business Cards

Why are business cards important?

You can often leave them at conference booths to win prizes and other goodies. But they're much more important than that.

As I mentioned in the previous section, business cards enable networking. They provide an easy way to exchange contact information and they reflect a certain level of professionalism. I've found this to be true even as technology has become important for networking (LinkedIn app anyone?)

LinkedIn and Business Cards

You should already have established your LinkedIn account and profile. This is true whether you're an experienced worker with many years in your profession or a newly minted professional who's just graduated. You should have a profile set up even if you aren't actively looking for a job. I've used mine to ask for input from colleagues or to try to find a contact at an organization.

You need that LinkedIn profile so that you can put the URL from your LinkedIn account on your business card.

It's an easy way to carry your resume around with you, and it actually offers a lot more space to promote your credentials. There are additional features, such as recommendations from others, that make LinkedIn even more valuable.

You'll see my LinkedIn URL in the right side of the image from my LinkedIn profile (on the next page). You'll notice that you can edit the URL. I'd recommend some version of your name. Once you've set this up, you can place this URL on your business cards.

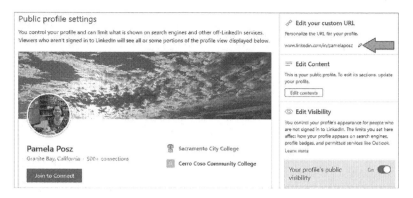

Where Can You Order Business Cards?

There are a variety of ways to buy or create your own business cards.

You can buy materials at an office supply store and print them yourself. This is a good solution if you realize you don't have any cards ready to go and you'll be attending a networking event in the immediate future, like tonight or tomorrow.

Office supply stores will also create business cards for you in a short time frame.

However, if you have any time to do this, I'd recommend that you order them online. There are a few websites that have some really attractive and fun designs for business cards and they won't cost a lot of money.

Here are my top choices:
• Moo.com
• Vistaprint.com
• Overnightprints.com

I personally love Moo.com because of the creativity of some of their designs. Overnightprints is probably the most inexpensive. Vistaprint has a lot of sales.

These and other similar sites offer multiple templates and designs that you can customize to your preference and create some amazing business cards without any design ability or experience. You can customize everything from the font to the paper.

Make sure that you choose paper stock that you can write on, even if it costs a little more money.

Some of these sites offer cards you can order for free. They usually have the logo of the website you ordered them from which is not a problem. However, the free cards are often printed on a type of paper that is hard to write on, which you'd want to avoid.

You always want to make sure that people can write notes on your card. If you meet a new person and start talking about something the other person may want to write down what you say on the back of the card in order to remember who said it. Business cards are also a convenient place to take a few short notes.

Make sure that there is space to write on the back of the cards and that you can do it with a normal pen and pencil.

When you're at the conference simply load up the conference badge holder with business cards. It makes them really easy to exchange because you don't have to dig them out of your bag, they're right there.

I also put any cards I collect in the badge holder as well. Just make sure you don't accidentally give out someone else's card that you were saving rather than your own.

You should make it a goal to exchange cards with at least 5 people you've never met whenever you attend a conference.

Contact After the Conference

Now that you've met all of these new people, you'll need to contact them.

You can either do this when you return home, or you can do this at the conference if you want to take care of it right away.

I like to use LinkedIn to maintain my network contacts. It's an easy way to contact people and as my network has grown, it's much easier to store information in LinkedIn than it is to add it to my work address book. I also know that my contacts will maintain their own information, so I don't worry that I'll lose track of anyone.

However, since everyone doesn't have a LinkedIn account, you may need to contact them via email and store their information in your contacts.

The Contact Email

Here's an example of an email you could write to make contact after the conference. You'll notice it's not very long. Keep the first message you send after the conference short and sweet. It will greatly increase the odds that your new contact will respond to the message.

Shandra,

It was a pleasure to meet you at the #### conference.

It was interesting to hear about ### (something you talked about with them at the conference).

We had a few interesting conversations about ###

OR

I sat next to you in the session on ### (if you remember where you met them at the conference). I just wanted to get in touch with you to make it easy for us to stay in contact.

Hopefully I'll see you at another time.

Sincerely,

Your Name
Email
Phone number
Small photo

Let's Review

- Don't go to a conference/workshop without business cards
- Make sure your LinkedIn account is up and running
- Order business cards online via a site like Moo.com or make them yourself
- Order cards with space on the back that you can write on with a normal pen/pencil
- Put your LinkedIn URL on your cards
- Exchange cards with at least 5 people at the conference
- Contact your new friends when you get home either via linked in or a simple email

Finally, for this section, let's look at how to do informational interviews, one of your best networking options.

2.9 Informational Interviews

I've given you multiple networking options that you may want to try. However, there is one that I've found to be particularly useful for connecting to people in your profession and increasing your network. It's the Informational Interview.

An informational interview is one of the best networking tools available to you. They provide direct connections to other professionals who may, in turn, be able to connect you to others. This is the reason that these interviews are particularly effective for anyone who is starting a new career. Additionally, when the job market is tight and there are multiple applicants for each job, personal connections like this can be very useful and may actually help you get hired.

What Is an Informational Interview?

An informational interview, in contrast to a job interview, is simply an appointment where you talk to someone to find out about their specific job and more generally about their career field. The appointment can be informal (having coffee with someone) or it can be more formal (meeting them in their office). You can also do an informational interview over the phone, although it won't be as effective as an in-person interview because networking works best with face to face contact.

The goal of an informational interview is not to specifically find out if there are any open positions, although this may come up naturally as part of the conversation. The best use of an informational interview is to learn about the day to day duties in a job or profession. And of course, the most important reason to do informational interviews is to professionally network with people working in that field.

Most people are friendly and happy to do this. It's also generally fun to hear about how people got started and what their job is actually like.

The Interview

The etiquette for informational interviews is that you should start by emailing your chosen interviewee to set up an appointment to meet face-to-face. You can also arrange a time to talk on the phone or use the Internet (such as Skype or Facetime) to connect. However, unless there's a substantial reason to use technology for the meeting, for example you don't live in the same area, I'd strongly suggest meeting in person. It will make more of an impression and you'll form a stronger connection. Make sure to communicate that the interview should only take about 30–45 minutes and that you understand the value of the interviewee's time.

Make sure to get a phone number for your interviewee in case of emergency. You'd need to call them if something came up that would prevent you from attending the meeting.

Prepare for the interview as you would for a somewhat less stressful job interview.

Come up with a list of questions you wish to ask. I've provided a few examples below. I'd suggest Googling "informational interview questions [your field]" to see if there are more specific questions relating to your field on the Internet. For example, if you were interested in going into nursing, you'd want to Google "informational interview questions nursing." Have extra questions prepared just in case the interview goes quickly. Identify the most important questions that you don't want to forget to ask. Don't forget to research the organization where the interviewee is employed. This should allow you to ask more relevant questions.

Dress appropriately (as if this were a job interview) and don't be late. Take your resume with you, but only provide it if you are asked.

You might want to bring some of the supplies I've listed for a job interview (see section 4.3). At a minimum you need to bring copies of your resume and pen and paper. You shouldn't take notes on your phone because it will seem to be rude and you may become distracted by your phone.

Make sure to completely turn off your phone before you start the meeting and put it out of site. If your phone is on, it's difficult to ensure that you've turned off all alerts. If they go off it can be embarrassing and distracting. You can turn it on again as soon as you finish.

Conduct the interview. Although you should make sure to ask questions, give your interviewee space to talk. Let the conversation develop organically.

Your final question should always be "Is there anyone else you would suggest I talk to?" This question transforms the experience from simply finding information about your field into a networking opportunity. It will provide you with your next professional connection. If you wanted to continue this experience you could then do an informational interview with the contact that your first interviewee provided.

If the interview has gone well, ask if you can connect to your contact on LinkedIn. This will allow you to stay in contact with them and make it easier to connect to their professional network.

Always thank your contact for their time before you leave.

As soon as possible after you finish, you need to send your thank you note. Although you may send a quick response via email you may also send a handwritten note or card. You may want to prepare this ahead of time and simply send it off after the interview. However, don't mail it until you've actually completed the interview. For example, it would be strange if you became ill and didn't show up but you'd already mailed the card.

Informational Interview Questions

Here are a few examples of questions you might ask during your interview. You need to tailor the questions to the interview depending upon who you are interviewing. Remember to do research ahead of time so you are somewhat familiar with the work environment of the person who you're going to interview.

- How did you get started in this field?
- What has your work history or career path been?
- How did you get to the position in which you are currently working?
- Could you explain the organizational structure of your organization?
- What would a typical day consist of?
- What did you do yesterday?
- What's the hiring process like?
- What are some of the skills and abilities necessary for someone to succeed in this job?
- What is the company's policy on providing seminars, workshops, and training so employees can keep up their skills or acquire new ones?
- What particular computer equipment and software do you use? Does this change very often?
- What kind of work can I expect to be doing the first year? How much will this change over time?
- What routine, detailed work will I encounter?
- How much guidance or assistance is made available to individuals in developing career goals?
- What organizations have you found helpful to participate in or network with?
- How often do you attend conferences or other career development activities?
- What professional organizations do you belong to?
- What should I wear to a job interview in this field?
- What educational path do I need to take to be successful in this field?
- Do you recommend any particular schools for my college education?

As I mentioned before, you can also Google "informational interview questions" to find more questions that you might want to ask. Add the name of the profession or job and you may get questions that are a little more specific to that field.

Chapter 3 – Your Application Materials

3.1 Be Prepared

Before I go into specifics about how to complete any of your application materials, let's look at how to set up a Job-Hunting Portfolio and why it's important.

Be Prepared to Apply for Jobs at Any Time

The slogan "Because every job is temporary" from the website Careerealism is true. Even if you think you'll never apply for another job, you cannot guarantee that this will happen. You may have to move unexpectedly or your ultimate dream job may suddenly be available. Be ready for it. This is particularly important because many employers cap the number of applications that they will accept or have a short application period. You need to have everything ready to go or you may miss the opportunity of your dreams.

Create a Job-Hunting Portfolio in a Binder

For a long time, I had all of my application materials from previous jobs stuffed into a few folders. I finally switched over to a binder with dividers and materials in sheet protectors. This has made it much easier to apply for jobs, particularly when the closing date comes up quickly. Everything I need is in one place and I am always ready to apply for any job in which I'm interested. My binder includes resumes, cover letters, old applications, transcripts, letters of recommendation and a few other odds and ends. I also have electronic versions of old application materials.

You will be far less stressed in your job hunt if you don't have to track down required information or documents at the last minute. This is particularly important when there is a lot of competition for jobs. Having a binder will ensure that you are always ready to apply for jobs. This simplifies everything and makes it easy to apply for any positions that interest you as soon as you see the advertisement or hear about the job.

Your Job-Hunting Portfolio

Your job-hunting portfolio should include:
- Cover Letters
- Resumes and/ or Curriculum Vitae
- List of References
- Letters of Recommendation
- Previous Applications
- High School Transcripts or diploma (if you are recently graduated)
- College Transcripts
- Examples of work you've done such as handouts or printouts of web pages
- Typing test certificate
- Business cards

Keep Print and Electronic Copies of Everything

Most employers require you to submit everything electronically. Pdfs are usually your best file format for submitting documents. They will retain any formatting you have created and the document will always look the same regardless of any computer and software differences.

If you have older printed versions of any of your documents, such as college transcripts, scan them to pdfs and have them ready to go. You don't want to have to scan your documents at the last minute.

Keep Print Copies of Your Old Applications

I have found it's particularly useful to keep print copies of every application I've ever filled out on file. You can always reconstruct information if you have a printout of your documents. The information required of applications seems to be a little different for every application. Once I've figured out the hourly wage of a job, it's nice not to have to figure it out again, particularly as time passes. I've also been thankful when an HR system has been updated, deleting a previous version of my application. Old copies of applications have saved me a huge amount of time over the years.

Keep copies of every application you've ever filled out. Different applications ask for the same information in different formats. For example, some applications may as for months of employment while others ask for days. Or some may ask for number of units while others ask for dates of enrollment. Once you've figure it out on one application, you don't want to have to do it again. You also want backups in case someone loses something that you submitted. I know that "the cloud" may seem to be the best option for storage for many things, but in this case, I'd actually keep hard copies of all documents.

Keep Screen Shots If You Don't Have Access to a Printer

If you don't have access to a printer, screen shots are an adequate backup, especially if you store them on multiple devices.

3.2 The Basics

Let's look at specific advice for filling out job applications.

Applications Can Be Really Important

Many job guides focus on cover letters and resumes, but I haven't seen as much advice about the importance of your application in your ability to get the job.

The application form itself can be just as important, if not more so, than any of the other materials you may submit, particularly with public sector jobs. In some cases, the first screening your materials go through is a review of your application. Your first chance to make an impression with a potential employer is often your application. If your application isn't perfect, you may be screened out. That well-crafted cover letter and resume may end up in the rejected folder if you submit a poor application.

Not all jobs require an application, but public sector jobs will generally require one.

Most applications can be filled out online. However, there are still occasional technological issues that come up.

Application Screening

If you know anyone at the organization to which you are applying, see if you can find out who is going to screen your application and adjust your process accordingly.

Application screeners may have to review hundreds of applications. If they are a manager or HR employee, they may constantly review applications. They are looking for easy ways to eliminate applications. Don't force them to eliminate yours by making simple mistakes or submitting an incomplete application. When I've screened applications, I become frustrated when someone submits a bad application. It's a waste of my time. Take the time to do it right.

The following are specific tips for the actual job application.

Don't Make the Screener Do the Extra Work

Don't make the screener connect the dots. For example, if you're mentioning your credentials of working with a diverse population and you mention that you have these skills, make sure to connect it to your experience.

Fill out the information on the application rather than writing in "see resume". If someone is screening hundreds of applications they may not flip back and forth between your application and your resume. Answer the questions on the actual application.

Neatness Hack

If, for any reason, you can't fill out the application on a computer you still need a way to keep your application neat even if your handwriting is not. Here's a somewhat nitpicky hack. Type out the answers to the application questions in a word processing document. Make sure your answers will fit in the spaces and adjust the font size as necessary. Print out this document and a copy of the application. Then cut out your answers with scissors and paste them on the copy of the application. Then scan or copy the application from the pasted copy you've made. This may sound like a lot of work but your application will be extremely neat and stand out from other applications. You can scan this as a .pdf and the formatting will hold.

Fill in every space, even if you have to say N/A (not applicable) or use a hyphen (–). If you leave a space blank it may appear as if you didn't answer the question.

Max Out Your Answers When You Can

Most areas in an application are short and specific, such as annual salary, name of employer, address. However, there are sometimes a few fields where you can write more information. For any fields where you can expand, add as much information as you can. You can often identify the areas of the application where it's possible to write longer answers because there's obviously a bigger space to write information. If you've written a paragraph and others have just written a sentence, you will be more likely to move forward in the process.

Look for the Supplemental Questions

Supplemental questions are often part of job applications and they can be extremely important.

In many cases, supplemental questions are added to the application when the institution can't change the generic job description. These often indicate specifics about what the employer is really looking for. Make sure to look for supplemental questions and answer them to the best of your ability. Although the word "supplemental" implies that they may be optional questions, they are not.

Watch for Health Requirements

Be sure that you meet the health requirements for the job. If a physical examination is a condition of employment, the employer must pay for it and can only request it after you are hired.

Do You Have a Misdemeanor or Felony?

Some applications request information about prior misdemeanor or felony convictions. Read the application questions carefully and answer truthfully, adding "will discuss at interview." You can be fired for not telling the truth on an application.

Common Errors to Avoid

These are common errors that will derail your application:

- Forgetting to sign the application
- Sending the application to the wrong address
- Missing the application deadline
- Entering an incorrect job tile and number

3.3 General Tips for All of Your Application Materials

Now let's look at more general tips that apply to all of your application materials including resumes, cover letters, as well as the application itself.

Check with Your References

Always talk to your references before beginning your job search, to ask permission to use their names, addresses, and phone numbers on your application(s). Former employers, business acquaintances, teachers, and the clergy are all acceptable references. Be sure to keep your reference list updated and let them know when you find a job.

You Are One of Many

Assume that there will be at least several hundred applicants for the job you want. If you had several hundred applications to review, including the application, resume and cover letter, how long would you take with each application the first time you reviewed them?

6 to 30 Seconds

Because of the large number of applicants, the HR representative may only review your application for 6 to 30 seconds for the first screening in order to decide if you will move forward in the hiring process or stop. You should assume that it will be really fast. Your materials must have an immediate impact in order to keep the reviewer reading so that you'll be screened in as an applicant. Everything should be perfect and you should try to stand out.

You Are Making an Impression

Even if you aren't hired for the job for which you are applying, you are laying groundwork for future applications. You may apply to the same organization more than one time. People remember the bad and good applications. If you make a poor first impression with your application materials, that may stick, even if you correct the problem later. Do it right the first time.

Strive for Perfection

Like all of your other materials, your application must be error free and complete, i.e. perfect. The quality of your application is often a screening criteria, which means that applicants are often screened out because of low quality submissions. Minor errors can cost you a job. Proper grammar and spelling are essential.

Make sure it's neat, that there are no errors, and that it is as complete as possible and that you've followed all instructions carefully. Employers will look at the quality of your application as a reflection of the quality of work they may expect out of you.

A good strategy is to read your materials out loud when you're proofing them. You may hear an error that you might otherwise have missed when you visually scan your materials.

I'd suggest that you also review paper copies of your application materials. You will often catch errors while reading a paper version that you might miss on a computer screen.

Other than any thank you notes do not submit handwritten materials.

Double check any names and titles. You will offend people if you get these wrong.

Follow Directions

Follow directions carefully. You will be judged on your ability to follow directions.

You will not move forward in the application process if you haven't followed directions carefully.

Include exactly what is listed in the job posting, no more or no less.

If the instructions say that you should submit just one letter of recommendation, do not send two.

Consistency counts. For example, if you start writing numbers out, continue writing them that way. If you start by writing 1,2,3... etc. continue that way. Don't switch in the middle. This also means that you should check for consistency before you submit your application.

Personalize Your Application Materials for the Specific Position

Apply for a specific position rather than a general job. This means that you should use keywords from the job posting in your application in order to personalize it. You can also change any lists of skills so that they are specific to the job for which you're applying.

Use Keywords From the Job Posting

The first screening of your materials may be completed by a computer. Make sure to use appropriate keywords that you pull from the position description. If you don't carefully choose your keywords, your application may never turn up in a search.

Avoid Abbreviations and Acronyms

Given that the HR department may screen your materials, you should spell out abbreviations and acronyms the first time they appear. The human resources staff may not be familiar with specifics of your profession or jargon from your field. This will avoid confusion.

Is Your Contact Info Current?

Make sure that all of your contact information (snail mail, email addresses, and phone numbers), are current. If your contact information changes contact Human Resources to let them know of the change.

As I've mentioned several times, you should have an email address for job hunting that contains your name. More on this in the next section.

Double-Check Dates

Make sure that your dates of employment make sense. For example, two full-time jobs should not have overlapping dates of employment. Make sure that they are listed in the correct chronological order, usually reverse chronological order.

Avoid Answering Any Preferred Salary Questions

If there's space for a desired salary, write negotiable or open. You should never discuss salary until you are offered the job.

How to Discuss Old Jobs with Class

Phrases to use to indicate why you've left a previous position:

- It was a temporary position
- The position ended
- The business closed
- The job contract ended
- Made a career change
- Went back to school
- Was laid off

Avoid the following phrases: quit, fired, tardiness

How to Discuss Volunteer and Internship Positions

List volunteer and internship positions in with the rest of your work experience. Simply label them as such.

Include Specifics

Include specifics whenever possible in all of your application materials. They will be much stronger than generalizations.

Example: Managed a book fair

Vs.

Managed a book fair which involved setting up the space, organizing volunteers, and maintaining an inventory of over 500 items. The school library profited with over $5000 from the fair, which could be used to purchase further library materials.

Specifics are much more powerful.

Highlight Technology

For many fields you should highlight technological skills wherever possible. This is true for all of your application materials. If there is a space to list the computer programs that you know how to use, make sure you list them.

Use the Active Voice

Use the active voice as much as possible in all of your application materials. Avoid using sentences that start with "I" or writing in the passive voice. For example: "This experience enabled me to..." or "Through my internship, I was responsible for...").

Start sentences with verbs.

Make yourself the subject of each sentence and use active descriptions (ex., "In this internship, I demonstrated sound judgment and problem–solving skills on a daily basis.").

Do not use contractions (I'd, didn't, it's).

Cover letters are a reflection of your writing skills, so make each cover letter an example of your best work.

3.4 Technology Issues

Technology Will Fail

Technology works all of the time... said no person ever.

At some point in your job search, you will struggle with technology. It's a major part of any job search. From the application, to your resume, to mapping your way to the interview, you will have to use technology. You can't avoid it.

The key with dealing with technology, particularly when outcomes are critical, is to assume that it will fail. Always have backups. Multiple backups.

One of best option for backups is actually print copies. Print copies won't become obsolete. They won't run out of power or storage. However, you should also keep multiple electronic copies of important documents in various locations. At this point cloud storage seems to be stable and secure. I have copies of everything in my Dropbox and Google accounts.

Set up an Email Address for the Job Hunt

If you don't already have an email address that is some version of your name, you need to create this account. It will be your main point of contact for your job hunt. You will use it for all documents and other information (such as websites) relating to your job hunt. For example, I created a Gmail address pamposz@gmail.com that I would use for a job hunt.

I would specifically recommend Gmail for this. As I've already mentioned, technology is now integral to most jobs. Even my dishwasher repairperson uses a laptop. You need to include technology in your application materials whenever possible. It may not seem to be important, but when hiring managers are looking at your resume and application for less than six seconds (the average time for resume review), even small things may indicate that you are tech savvy.

Control Your File Names

In order to make it easy to find your documents, include your name whenever you name a document. For example, [Your Name] resume and [Your Name] cover letter.

Scan the Documents Yourself

If you only have printed copies of your application materials and you need to submit electronic versions, make sure to scan them yourself. HR departments will sometimes offer to scan your materials for you. In my experience, the quality of scans done by HR departments is lower than that done by the person submitting the application. For example, sometimes the scans were incomplete or the pages looked strange. Do the scan yourself.

What Electronic Format Should You Use for Your Files?

Once you've created your resume, you should have a version that is a pdf file and another version that is an rtf file.

A .pdf (portable document file) will hold all formatting you use and works well if you know that a person will print out and look at the version of your resume that you have submitted electronically.

A .rtf file (rich text format) is a text file that will hold the formatting you have created in your resume. It looks like any other word processing document, such as an MS Word file. However, it also works well with a variety of different word processing applications because it is a cross platform format. If you use rtf, you do not have to worry that you don't have the most current version of a word processor which would mean that the HR person won't be able to read your resume and application materials. An rtf file works well when you know that someone will want to copy text from your resume. They may not be able to do that with a pdf.

Most current word processors allow you to choose either of these formats when you save your document. Simply choose Save As and you should find either of these formats for your application materials.

A Scannable Resume

If you are mailing a print copy of your resume, you might want to find out if the HR department will be scanning your resume into a computer or a database. The following are formatting tips you might want to use to ensure that your resume will scan electronically.

Leave white spaces between sections of the resume so the computer can read it easily.

Print only on one side of the paper.

Use KEYWORDS and phrases that are commonly used in your career field to describe your skills and experience.

Do not fold the resume. Mail the resume in a large envelope with extra postage.

Keep the design simple; words, not pictures.

Prepare resume on white paper.

Do not bold, italicize, or underline any information.

Use a size 12 simple font (such as: Arial, Courier, or Helvetica).

Do not use hollow bullets.

Do not use symbols such as the number (#) sign.

Do not use tables.

If you can submit a formatted version – you should do so. It's much easier to read. Save the .txt format when there are no other options.

Test Your Materials on Different Devices

This advice particularly applies to your resume. You should test how your resume appears on different devices to make sure nothing strange happens with the formatting. I would check it on both iPhone and Android phones, iPad, and a regular computer. If you've saved it as a pdf, check that version on the different devices as well.

3.5 It's the Math

This section largely applies to the application process for public sector, i.e. government jobs.

Equity in the Hiring Process

Public sector hiring is different than private sector hiring because it is controlled by equity. Equity means that everyone is treated the same way from the application through the interview. Most public agencies go to great lengths to ensure that the process is equitable and fair to all candidates. In order to make sure that all applicants are treated the same there are strict processes that govern everything and an increased level of bureaucracy throughout all HR processes. The applications must be screened the same way. Interviews must be conducted the same way.

For public sector jobs you will literally be scored on your application and your interview. Understanding how the math works is really important for your potential success.

Throughout the hiring process, all of your application materials, including your interview, are given a numeric score and ranked against the other applicants. Your application and interview scores control whether you will be interviewed, whether you move on to the next interview round and whether you are hired. It is important that you understand how math may affect this process because it will affect your ability to get the job.

Screening Your Application

Screening starts when you submit your application packet, which usually includes an application, resume, cover letter, letters of recommendation, and academic transcripts. All of these documents will be screened and scored based on a set of specific criteria.

A common screening criterion for applications is the quality of your application. If your application packet is messy or incomplete or even if you submit extra materials because you're not following the directions, you may not receive any points for one section. This will lower your score and you may be screened out of the candidate pool simply because of your application, rather than your qualifications. Your application should always be perfect and you need to follow all directions carefully. Always have at least one other person check your application for errors before you submit it to make sure that there are no errors or mistakes with your application.

Interview Scoring Example

Let's specifically look at how scoring works in an interview.

For this example, there are a total of eight interview questions.

The candidates are scored from 0 to 5 for each question.

Zero is the low score, five is the high score.

Let's start by looking at the scores of two of the candidates, Candidate 1 and Candidate 2. There are two scenarios for Candidate 2:

In scenario A Candidate 2 completely missed Question 2.

In scenario B Candidate 2 gave an average answer for Question 2, not a great answer, just average.

In **Scenario A** Candidate 2 did not miss any questions and scored three points higher than Candidate 1. Candidate 2 would be ranked higher.

In **Scenario B**, Candidate 2 generally did better than Candidate 1 and scored higher on more of the questions. However, because Candidate 2 completely missed Question 2 and received a 0 on that question, the overall score of Candidate 2 is lower than Candidate 1. Candidate 1 would be ranked higher because they did not fail at one specific question.

Here's the actual scoring:

Interview Questions	Candidate 1	Candidate 2	
		Scenario A	Scenario B
1	5	5	5
2	3	5	0
3	3	4	4
4	3	4	4
5	4	4	4
6	3	4	4
7	4	4	4
8	4	3	3
9	4	4	4
	33	37	32

"Above the Line" and "Below the Line"

Scoring becomes even more important when we look at the ranking of all of the interview candidates together.

Candidates are often grouped by their scores to decide who will move forward in the hiring process. Two of the most common ways to do this are to continue with a certain number of the top candidates, such as the top three; or to continue with those who achieve a minimum score or higher.

In either case, candidates will be ranked above or below the line.

Those who are "above the line" will move forward in the hiring process.

Those who fall "below the line" will not move forward in the hiring process.

Scenario A – Candidate Moves Forward

Let's continue to look at the scores of Candidate 2 in comparison to the complete pool interview candidates.

In Scenario A, Candidate 2 moves forward in the hiring process because they didn't completely miss any of the questions.

Scenario A		
Candidate	**Score**	
10	40	**Above the Line**
7	38	**∗∗∗**
5	38	**Moves**
2	37	**Forward**
4	36	
1	33	**Below the**
6	29	**Line**
8	29	**∗∗∗**
9	28	**Doesn't Move**
3	25	**Forward**

Scenario B – Missed One Question – Doesn't Move Forward

In Scenario B, even though Candidate 2 generally did better at all of the question, their score falls below the line simply because they missed one question completely. They will not move forward in the hiring process.

This is true regardless of whether the hiring committee selects the top five candidates or whether they select everyone with a score of 35 and above. Either are common ways to select the job candidates who will move on in the hiring process.

Scenario B		
Candidate	Score	
10	40	Above the Line
7	38	***
5	38	Moves
4	36	Forward
1	33	Below the
2	32	Line
6	29	***
8	29	Doesn't Move
9	28	Forward
3	25	

The Takeaway

Here's the takeaway for all of this information.

Don't completely mess up one of the interview questions so that you receive a zero on that question.

It is the equivalent of flunking one test in a class. Even if you don't have a good answer to an interview question, say something. **Completely missing one interview question can cost you the job even if you did well otherwise.**

3.6 Proofing Your Application Materials

One of my main pieces of advice for all of your application materials is proof, proof, proof, proof... you get the idea. Always proof your materials multiple times before you submit them.

Your materials must be flawless. If you have any mistakes with your materials you will not move forward in the application process. I refer to this as going into the round file, i.e. the trash can.

Proofing any materials you submit can be one of the most critical steps when you are applying for a position.

Make Sure to Run a Spelling and Grammar Check

You need to eliminate common errors. However, having said that....

Do Not Rely Completely on Spell Check

I once had a virus in my resume that inserted the word "wazzu" at random points in the document. I can't imagine that Pamela wazzu Posz would be hired even with my wazzu expertise in Microsoft Word and wazzu Excel. Spell check did not pick up wazzu. I only noticed wazzu by reviewing the print copy of my documents.

Additionally, if you've ever accidentally added a word to the dictionary in your computer, spell check will not find it. The grammar in resumes is somewhat strange and can confound grammar check.

Review a Print Copy

After you have saved your documents, print them out in order to check the formatting. You will catch certain things you may miss on screen such as the fact that your printer won't print the bottom ½ inch of your resume, or weird spacing between bullets.

Reading your materials aloud is another very effective way to catch errors. You will hear things that don't work or are incorrect that you might have missed if you only view it on a screen.

You should also print out your materials and check the formatting after you have saved it as a .pdf to make sure that nothing has changed.

If you can't print it out or don't have access to a printer – at least print it to pdf. This will freeze the formatting and make it more likely that you'll catch errors. You can also send this to others to proof, which brings me to...

Have Others Proof Your Materials

Make sure to have several other people review print copies of your application materials. I often advise students to have five people look at them. Make sure to provide your reviewers with the position description that you are applying for. This will allow them to better assess whether your application matches the position.

If you are not a native English speaker have a native English speaker review your materials if at all possible.

3.7 Resumes

This section will cover many specific tips that you can use to create the resume that will get you the interview.

What Is a Resume?

"The resume is a selling tool that outlines your skills and experiences so an employer can see, at a glance, how you can contribute to the employer's workplace."[14]

Your resume is not the kitchen sink, it shouldn't include everything. You are highlighting positives from your experience, skills, abilities, and qualifications.

You will not get the job based purely on your resume. The purpose of your resume (and other application materials such as your cover letter) is to get you an interview.

However, your resume will leave a lasting impression. If you have an excellent resume, it conveys all of the information you wish to convey about your job history. If it's a really good resume, it can also convey attention to detail and the quality of your work.

Who Will See Your Resume?

Be aware that your resume may be initially reviewed and screened by a human resources person. You may want someone outside the profession to review it who can tell you if it's general enough to be understandable or if there's too much jargon.

Six Seconds

As I mentioned in the section on application materials, the HR professional may only take six seconds to review your resume.

If you'd like to experience what this would be like, try the 6 Second Resume game from the website Resume Genius.[15] You'll spend six seconds each reviewing 10 resumes and decide which you would keep and which you would toss. The website also explains which resumes are the best choice so you can see the entire process.

How Do You Know Your Resume Is Working?

Remember that the purpose of your resume is to get an interview. When you start to get interviews, you know that you have a good starting resume.

Updating Your Resume

You will need to periodically update your resume to keep it up to date provide an accurate reflection of your work history. Moving to a new position, completing a new level of education, and finishing a major project are all common reasons to update your resume. You can also simply update it every few years. Remember that it is much easier to remember the details of a job when it is fresh. When you switch to a new position, remember to update the section about your old position. Have you learned something new on the job? Add that. Even if you don't keep track of all of this information in the full format of your resume, in proper resume language, make some notes that will help you remember what you were doing and enable you to reconstruct it later.

3.7.2 Create a Master Resume

Are you stressed just looking at the title of this section? Not sure about where to start? How do I create a master resume? That sounds like a lot of work.

Don't worry. This section will break the work down into smaller steps which will make it as painless as possible.

Just start writing it down, don't worry about formatting, I'll go over that shortly.

You can always edit the document after you've listed all of the information.

Managing Your Time and Getting Started

You don't have to do this in one sitting. If that stresses you out too much, do one step or 10 minutes per night until you're finished. Or you may want to set aside a big block of time in case you get momentum going and want to knock most/all of it out in one sitting.

The hardest part may be simply starting. I know that with projects like this, I often simply need to get started, then I build momentum and flow and the rest is easier. If you are avoiding this and have a hard time getting started, try to write something/anything (it doesn't even have to relate to your resume) just to get something written down. Spend about 5 minutes writing to get some flow going. Once there's something on the page/computer screen and the screen is no longer blank and overwhelming, then start working on your resume.

Formatting

Don't worry about properly formatting your resume when you start this process. You can do that after you've written down all of the information you will include in the master resume. Save formatting for last. I'll cover formatting later.

At this point, you simply want to create a text document that will serve as the basis for a specific resume. You can format after you have written down all/most of the information.

Why Create a Master Resume?

Before we go into the how, let's look at the why.

One of the most common pieces of advice I see relating to job hunting, is that you should tailor your application materials, which would include your resume, to the specific job for which you are applying. Creating a master resume is the easiest way to prepare for applying to a variety of different positions.

Most importantly though, once you've created a master resume you will always be prepared to apply for any position. You won't have to scramble to add positions to your resume at the last minute.

It prepares you for any type of position for which you wish to apply, with little or no notice. This is particularly important because many job postings will only accept the first 50/100/200 applications. You need to have something ready to go at any time.

Additionally, a master resume will also be useful for filling out applications because you'll have your complete job history in one document.

This is also one of the best ways to create the information you'll use

How to Create a Master Resume

If you've never created any sort of resume, you're in luck. This exercise will provide you with a big resume that you'll be able to tailor to any position.

I'll break this down into small steps. Hopefully, this will be less overwhelming.

Don't worry about how long this is. It should be a multi-page document. You can edit it down later.

You don't have to follow the order I list below, but you should complete each of the steps. If you remember your position titles more than the places you worked, start your list with your position titles. Start with whatever is easiest in order to get momentum going.

With education, work experience and anything else that has a chronological order, you'll need to list it in reverse chronological order with the most recent options first and going backwards.

With your work history, one of the main goals is to avoid any holes in your resume. If you were out of the job market for a while, try to think of anything you could include as an alternative. For example, did you volunteer or work on any projects? Did you start your own business? If you're having problems with this, talk to friends and family to see if you've missed or forgotten anything that might be relevant.

Start by creating one giant generic outline that you can use to pull all of your information together in one document. You will then have a complete listing of everything you've done. This list is also useful when you need to fill in your employment history on a job application. You should also track down all of those details you may not remember such as names of supervisors, addresses and phone numbers.

When you actually apply for jobs you will edit down your resume and just include the sections that relate to the job for which you are applying. For many positions you should try to edit it down to 1 page.

If you know that you'll be applying for certain categories of jobs (such as public service or technical service positions), you could create a generic resume for each category.

All of this may seem like a lot of work, but if you do it at one time, you'll save yourself a lot of work in the long run and you can add on to the document as time passes. Before we get into content, let's look at the language you should use in your resume.

3.7.3 Tailoring Your Resume

Create a one-page Resume from your master resume.

Figure out the most likely positions to which you'll apply and create a smaller resume specifically for that type of position.

This just means you'll edit the master resume down for this particular type of position.

Look for keywords you might want to include.

Edit down positions that are duplicates. You will still want to include basic information about the position to avoid holes in your resume. But you don't need to include as much information about the duplicate position.

How do I tailor a generic resume for a specific position?

Make sure to keep a copy of any ads for positions you have applied for. If you get an interview, you will want to refer back to the original job listing in order to prepare for the interview.

Review section 1.4 for a complete explanation of reviewing the job listing.

3.7.4 Specific Resume Sections

How to Describe Your Duties

List the position title first for any jobs you are describing – that's what you're trying to emphasize. Then list the location and date.

Your Work History

Start by simply listing the places where you worked.

Make the list as complete as possible.

Add the names of all of the positions you've held.

Try to get the positions titles as correct as possible. If you aren't sure what to use – do a little online research into your previous employers. Check LinkedIn or do a general Internet search to find the correct position titles at companies in your work history.

Add the years and then months of your employment. As with everything else, this should be as accurate as possible.

Ask friends, relations, current and former co–workers for help if you're having a hard time creating this time line.

Make a list of your duties at each place of employment. Include everything you can remember. Don't worry about how it's written at this point, just include everything you did.

Your Education

Add your education. Where did you go to school? What was your major? What is the official name of your degree? (You may have to Google this – or look at your diploma or transcripts).

Include any training programs or certifications you have earned.

Make sure you have the correct names of your courses and degrees.

If you took one or two college courses, I would not include them on your resume.

If you have completed most of the coursework for a degree, you will want to include it.

Example:

Coursework in Anthropology and Art – University of California Davis – – 2010–2013

If you've almost completed your degree:

Bachelor of Arts – Art and Anthropology

University of California, Davis – Expected Completion – May 2015

Until you've completed your degree, you may want to include specific coursework on your resume. The most relevant coursework to the position should be listed first. List the actual name of the course. For example, use Introduction to Psychology rather than the course designator, Psych 300.

If you have a degree:

Bachelor of Arts – Art and Anthropology

University of California, Davis – December 2005

Skills and Qualifications

Do you speak/read/understand any foreign languages?

Add them.

Are there any other skills or abilities you want to include?

If you're having a hard time, you can always look at the resumes of others online to see if there's anything else you wish to add.

Make sure to focus on any jobs you've held that may have relevant skills. Make a list of all of your skills and strengths.

Make a list of your accomplishments (such as any awards or scholarships you may have received), particularly the ones that demonstrate your skills and strengths.

Technology

Make a list of every type of hardware and technology you know how to use. For example, if you were applying for a job in a public library you would want to include the names of any e-readers that you know how to use.

Make a list of every type of software you are familiar with. Make sure you spell them correctly and use correct punctuation, capitalization and spelling. PowerPoint, Facebook, iTunes are examples of names that may use capitalization differently.

With both the hardware and the software, list all programs and hardware you can think of that you know how to use, even if you aren't as familiar with some. You can always add a designation to indicate proficiency; for example, expert user, familiar with, etc.

Internship and Volunteer Positions

Internship and volunteer positions belong in your resume with the rest of your work experience.

You can build an entire resume out of volunteer work if you don't have any other experience. Many of these positions have a lot of responsibility which looks good on a resume. This also demonstrates that you were willing to give of your time without financial compensation.

Add these positions where they fit chronologically when you're creating your list of positions. These can be particularly important if you have been out of the work force for a while or if you are changing careers and you need to fill in chronological gaps in your work experience. If you don't need to fill a gap in your work history and your resume is already fairly long, you may want to include them in a separate section.

You must label them as volunteer work or internships.

I would rank an internship over a volunteer position. In general, internships are more official and structured and have a much higher level of accountability than volunteer work. I'll discuss this more in the section on internships.

Volunteer work is particularly strong if you started out as a volunteer for an organization and then you moved into a paid position. This means that someone liked you enough after working with you to actually hire you. If you have been hired from a volunteer position or internship list these as two separate positions.

3.7.5 Resume Language

Use regular language, nothing too grandiose or inflated. Keep it simple.

Use the active voice.

Use Verbs

Every sentence in your experience should start with a verb.

Be specific about what you did in a position.

Break it down – don't just make a generic statement. "I ran a library" doesn't really say much about what you did. You need to list specific duties you performed. Here are a few examples I pulled from a student resume that demonstrate what I'm talking about. You'll also notice the use of numbers which is really strong and would stand out.

* Performed technical and administrative functions; ordering, receiving, cataloging, managing
  material
* Assisted patrons in person and by telephone with requests for materials, circulation questions,
  patron records, fines, lost materials
* Provided reference assistance to teachers and students
* Increased Charles Mack Library hours and use by 29%
* Maintained proper functioning of media resources
* Planned, organized, and hosted first Library Book Fair which sold over $4,600

Make sure the tenses of your verbs match when you worked in a place – i.e. if it is a past position – it all should be in past tense. If you are still in the job, it should all be in the present tense.

Make sure your sentences aren't too long. If you don't know how to deal with clauses – break them into smaller sentences. It will be easier to read and less likely that you'll have to deal with complicated punctuation.

Make sure you have the correct names for things – Certificate of Achievement – Library and Information Technology, Associate in Science – Library and Information Technology.

Check your spelling – cataloging not cataloguing. Don't forget to do this for software products. If you are applying for a position in a foreign country you should use the spelling rules of that country. For example, if you are applying for a position in Great Britain, you would use grey instead of gray, colour instead of color.

Make sure you have the correct name for your degree.

Make sure you have the correct name for any software programs you list. For example, ProQuest has that capital Q in the middle. Google the items you aren't sure about to get the correct information.

3.7.6 Formatting and Layout

Tables make it easy to control the formatting of your resume. Set up all of your text in tables. This will allow you to easily control alignment with all of your sections.

Start with the table borders visible so that you can see everything.

Once you have formatted the document you can hide the borders of the table.

Don't use tables if you are creating a mobile–ready resume. They will not display correctly on a cell phone.

Although tables can help with formatting, make sure that they won't cause problems. There are some online systems that won't display the information in tables.

Fonts

FONTS ARE IMPORTANT
CHOOSE CAREFULLY

To be or not to be

TO BE OR NOT TO BE

To be or not to be

To be or not to be

To be, or not to be,
That is the question

There are a lot of people who really care about fonts so make sure to choose your font wisely. I like Cambria (serif font) and Calibri (sans-serif font).

Do not use Times New Roman unless the instructions tell you to use this font. Nothing says 1990s like Times New Roman.

Avoid Italics

Italics come across as tentative which is not what you're going for on your resume. Never use italics in your resume.

The Heading

Both your cover letter and your resume should have the same heading.

Set up the heading with your personal information as a header – it's easier to match formatting across the documents. This should include your name, address, phone number and the email address that has your name (which you should set up for job hunting).

Your name is the one item on the resume that can be in a different font to make it stand out. Everything else should use the same font.

Job Hunting Email Address

This is just a reminder that you should set up a specific email address with your name for the job hunt. As I mentioned in section 3.4, Technology Issues, it should be a Gmail address that includes your name.

3.7.7 Resume Don'ts – Things to Avoid

Do not include an objective. Most objectives are versions of "I want a great position at a great company" which is not what employers are looking for. They also often take up space you could use more effectively in other ways. If you do have space, you might include a summary statement instead of an objective.

You might want to include a summary statement at the top of your resume. These have replaced objectives, which you do not want to include.

Here's an example: An easy going, yet hard working librarian with over 15 years of experience helping library users.

I enjoy figuring out how to use technology to improve service for library users.

My design skills and ability to think creatively have been an asset to every place I've worked.

Do not use clichés. They can actually hurt your chances of moving forward with your application because they've been used so much and don't really mean anything. "Good with people" is an example that comes to mind. Instead using generic clichés, explain how you actually did the work. For example, "Assisted patrons with the library databases enabling them to find eBooks and articles and either print or download or email them for later use," is much stronger than "Good with people." You might want to Google resume clichés, resume mistakes or resume language to avoid to make sure you haven't used these on your resume.

Avoid using jargon. Your resume will often start out in the HR department and they may not be familiar with library jargon. You can compensate for this to a certain extent by listing items in categories that will help someone outside the field understand what you're talking about, particularly with technology. For example, you could list a group of database names if you include library databases as a category name.

Do not use abbreviations (with the possible exception of technological names).

Do not include anything that you didn't actually do – i.e. don't lie.

Don't use "etc." If there are more items you should list them all.

Do not use "References available upon request."

Do not include hobbies or other activities you like to do when you're not at work.

3.7.8 Bad Resume Example

This is an example of a poorly formatted and designed resume.

Compare this with the next section for the good version of this resume.

A few of the problems with this resume:

Errors (such as the lack of capitalization in the header)

Bad email address and too much information in the header

Inclusion of an Objective (it adds nothing)

Poorly formatted education

Lack of information about work experience

References are listed on the resume

Times New Roman font is dated

Rose quartz
555 Envelope Lane, Beach City, California, 94959
ilovesteven@hotmail.com
916-222-0055

Objective: To obtain an Associate Degree in Occupational Therapist.

Education: Smithson Anglican School   1979 - 1992

           Roberta's Commercial School   1993 – 1997

           University of New South Wales   2002 - 2004

Summary of Qualification:

Pitman Examination Institute: Typewriting – Advanced   1994

           Shorthand Speed 50 w.p.m   1993

Australian Examination Council:

Office Procedures	Grade I	1995
Principles of Accounts	Grade I	1996
Principles of Business	Grade I	2007
Mathematics	Grade II	2017

The Computer Instruction & Research Centre: Successfully completed a Computer Literacy Programme - 1995

Successfully completed Studies in Administrative Professional Secretaryship (APS), with the University of the New South Wales School of Continuing Studies: 2002 - 2004
Working Experience:
Division of Education, Youth Affairs & Sports
Goodwoman High School
Clerk Typist   1998 – 2006

New South Wales Regional Health Authority
Secretary – Human Resource Department
11th December, 2006 to 31st December, 2008

New South Wales Regional Health Authority
Executive Administrative Assistant
2nd January, 2009 to August, 2018
Community Involvement
Member of the Seventh Day Adventist Pathfinder Club
References:
Yellow Diamond Destiny
yellow.diamond@gmail.com
925-111-3259

Jasper Schmoobert
jasper.schmoo45@nswu.edu

3.7.9 Good Resume Example

This is an example of a well formatted and designed resume.

It's easy to visually scan in a short time. You get a clear picture of the work history of Rose Quartz in a matter of moments.

Why is this version better than the previous version?

Lack of errors

Good document header

Alignment of information makes it easy to read

The names of the degrees are highlighted

Four qualities are highlighted with the skills and qualifications

Bulleted list of skills and qualifications

Work experience is well formatted

Job titles in bold

Action verbs used to describe job duties

The table cell borders would be invisible in the final version. However, you can see here how they help control the formatting and alignment of the document.

ROSE QUARTZ
916-222-0055 | rose.quartz11@gmail.com

Education:	Associate Degree – Administrative Professional Office Management University of New South Wales	2017
	Certificate – Administrative Professional Secretaryship University of New South Wales	2004
Skills & Qualifications:	**Goal Oriented, Organized, Team Player** **Strong Customer Service Skills** • Typing 70 WPM • Shorthand 40 WPM • MS Word, PowerPoint, Excel, Publisher, Outlook • Gmail, Google Drive, Sheets, Slides, Docs • Dropbox	
Experience:	**Executive Administrative Assistant** New South Wales Health Authority (NSWHA) Port Stephens, New South Wales, Australia • Took minutes at meetings run by NSWHA Operations Manager • Managed reporting system from various departments in the Operations Division • Assisted in management of office enabling the Operations Manager to function effectively • Maintained schedule of Operations Manager • Scheduled meetings with NSWHA Department Heads • Collected and collated information for presentations	Jan 2009 – Aug 2018
	Secretary New South Wales Regional Health Authority Port Stephens, New South Wales, Australia • Took minutes at meetings run by Human Resources Department • Assisted in management of office enabling the Human Resources Manager • Collected and collated information for presentations	Dec 2006 – Dec 2008
	Clerk Typist Division of Education, Youth Affairs & Sports Goodwoman High School • Assisted in management of school office enabling administrators, teachers, and students to function successfuSlly	Sep 1998 – May 2006

3.8 Cover Letters

General Tips

Keep your letter short and simple. This is not the time to tell your life story.

I would generally recommend that you write the resume first and then write the cover letter based on your resume. If it's important enough to mention in the cover letter, it should be on your resume. In other words, don't include information in your cover letter that isn't also reflected in your resume.

Research the company and the specifics about the position so you can tailor your letter to the needs of the organization.

Include information that is specific to the job for which you are applying. Your letter will be less generic and will make a better impression.

Be sure to sign your letters. (Black ink is suggested)

Use the Same Header in all of your Application Materials

I've stated this before, but it bears repeating here. Your resume and cover letter should both have the same header.

Addressing Your Letter

If possible, write to someone specific. Unsolicited letters often get lost. In the public sector, sending letters and e-mails to the head of the organization will not directly lead to a job. You need to apply to a specific job that has been posted.

If you do not have the correct information, call the employer to get the correct name and spelling, the title, and address, email, or fax number.

Write each cover letter specifically for the company and/or position you are seeking. If you let the person know the position right up front it is more likely to get to the right person.

If you do not have a name and you are applying for a specific advertised position, you may use the following without a salutation:

Re: Sales position (include position number if there is one)

OR

Dear Ms. XXX: (if you can get the name, but don't know if it the right person)

I am interested in the position of Sales Associate that was recently advertised on your website.

Body of the Letter

I'd recommend using a T format cover letter. They are easy to review and easier to write than a traditional letter.

Here's the format.

First Paragraph

The first paragraph is the same as a traditional cover letter format.

Start with a friendly opening. Include a reminder of any prior contacts, if any. Mention the reason for your correspondence. Begin with the purpose of your letter, stating the specific position or type of work you seek. If you were referred to the addressee, indicate by whom, using the name of a contact or mutual acquaintance.

Response Section

After the first paragraph you copy the requirements from the position description and line them up on the left. Then you respond to each of them (or as many as possible) with how you meet that requirement.

Follow Up Paragraph

After you list the responses to everything, you can write a general paragraph adding anything else you'd like to highlight.

Closing Paragraph

Close with an action statement. Clearly identify what you will do next. Do not leave it up to the employer to contact you, since that doesn't guarantee a response. Close on a positive note and let the employer know you desire further contact.

Request the next step in the employment process: an interview.

If possible, indicate that you will contact the addressee at a specific date or time to arrange a mutually convenient appointment time.

You may request a written response especially if the organization is not local.

Be positive in your attitude; expect an appointment or a response.

T Style Cover Letter Example

Here's an example of a t–style cover letter. The requirements were pulled directly from the job advertisement. The dotted lines won't appear in the final version.

ROSE QUARTZ
916-222-0055 | rose.quartz11@gmail.com

January 25, 2020
Makerspace Lab Coordinator Assistant Position (#123459)
Metropolis City College
5151 Capital Ave.
Metropolis, CA 95822

To the Selection Committee:

I am applying for the Makerspace Lab Coordinator - Assistant (20%) position. In my current position as Library Program Coordinator and Librarian, and with my many years of experience at Metropolis City College, and a personal connection to the Makerspace, I am ideally qualified for this position. I offer the following qualifications in response to the requirements of this position:

Your Requirements	My Qualifications
High degree of organization	My current position as Coordinator of the Library Program requires a high degree of organization. For example, I typically mentor and supervise over 20 student internships each semester I also plan and conduct several annual events.
Ability to work creatively and productively with a variety of people	I have many years of positive experience working with a diverse range of people, including students, faculty, staff, administrators, and members of the public from different social, economic, cultural, ideological, racial and ethnic backgrounds.
Demonstrated ability to develop, implement, and evaluate projects in a timely manner	I have a strong history of developing, implementing, completing, and evaluating projects.
Ability to develop and monitor a budget	I plan and maintain a budget as the Coordinator of the Library Program.
Ability to plan and facilitate meetings among diverse constituency groups	I have many years of experience running meetings which includes the following tasks: recruiting members, planning the agenda, and scheduling the meeting.

I have used these qualifications while working at the Metropolis City College Library and other libraries in the Sacramento region. On a personal level, I am a creative, hardworking professional with the proven ability to learn new duties easily and adapt to a wide variety of new technologies. I truly enjoy working in the educational environment of community colleges in California and interacting with such a diverse group of students, patrons, and colleagues. I look forward to interviewing with you soon.

Sincerely,

Rose Quartz

3.9 Professional Letters of Recommendation

There are a variety of situations where you may need to ask someone to serve as a reference for you or write you a letter of recommendation. For the most part these will be references for a job or applications for school and you would contact an instructor, employer or mentor.

Don't be shy about asking for a recommendation if you have done "A" level work. People are usually happy to help out others in these situations. If I like a student, employee or coworker and feel that they've done an excellent job, I'm always happy to help someone out by serving as a reference or writing a letter of recommendation. I remember how happy I was when people offered to do this for me.

As with everything else, there is etiquette for these types of requests.

Always Ask First

Always ask before you list someone as a reference. Don't assume that they will be willing to do this if you haven't talked to your reference first. Additionally, they will be much better prepared to answer questions about you if you let them know when they may expect to get a call about you.

Ask for a Letter Before You Leave a Position

If you are going to leave a position and feel that your work has been good, ask for a letter before you go. Your reference can write you a generic letter of recommendation that you can use in your job hunt. Don't let time pass before you ask for a letter because the letter will be much stronger and more detailed if you have recent contact with your reference. If you wait until time has passed, the letter will not be as strong as it would be if you requested it within a short time frame.

Ask for a Letter When the Class Is Over

If you are a high school or college student and you have done well in the class (i.e. received an A), consider asking your teacher for a letter of recommendation when the class is over. As with leaving a position, you should do this as soon as possible after the class has ended. If too much time has passed, the instructor is much less likely to remember you and your work. I would only ask for a letter from an instructor if you have done well in the class.

Your Letters Should Be Recent

You should submit fairly recent letters of recommendation. In most cases, if you don't have any recent references or letters of recommendation, this will reflect poorly on you and may affect your chances of getting the interview (if they ask for letters ahead of time) or the job (if they check your references). Your application will not be as strong if all of your references are 5 or more years old. This means that you should continue to develop new references and keep in touch with previous references as you progress in your career. You can also contact old references and ask for an updated letter if you need a more recent version.

References from sources other than jobs and school are also perfectly acceptable references, particularly when the skills

128

transfer to the work for which you are applying. For example, if you were out of the workforce but volunteered regularly, you could ask your volunteer supervisor or other volunteers to provide you with a reference.

If you don't have a recent letter or reference, you need to find a way to get one. Find someone you work with, within your organization that you can ask for a letter of recommendation or reference. If you don't want your current employer to know that you are looking for a job, choose your reference wisely and communicate the fact that this is private information. They may accidentally share the information if you don't make this clear.

What If They Say No?

If a person refuses your request, say thank you and move on. You probably don't want a letter of recommendation from someone who has reservations or concerns about your work. The letter they would provide is likely to be negative or really basic and in either case isn't likely to improve your application. Find someone else to recommend you who is willing to talk about you in glowing terms.

This is a situation where I would not ask for feedback about why you didn't get the letter. You may make the person uncomfortable and/or angry which will not help you in your pursuit of a job, particularly because they may have a professional connection to the job or situation for which you are applying. The library world is a small place. You never know who is personally or professionally connected. Simply thank them for their time and move on.

Make the Request via Email

Email is the best way to make these requests for a number of reasons.

It will allow you to spend some time crafting a nice formal request and this is a situation that calls for a higher level of formality than you might normally use. Even if you are friends with your reference, I would aim for a more formal request.

I have found that most people are less stressed by doing this via email rather than in person. When you use email, you can spend more time crafting your request. Additionally, if the person doesn't wish to serve as one of your references, it's considerably less awkward to either reject someone or receive a rejection via email than in person.

Email also offers the advantage that if the person receives a lot of requests, it will be easier for them to keep track of each request.

If you still wish to make the request in person, make sure to do so in private when there aren't any other people around. I have had students ask me for a letter in front of other people. If I didn't wish to provide a letter of reference, I am either forced to lie to them to avoid an uncomfortable situation, or say no which is also extremely awkward.

What Is the Letter For?

Make sure to let your reference know what you need the letter for. They'll be able to tailor it to different situations and create a much stronger recommendation.

Is it a generic letter of recommendation? These letters aren't for a specific position or application, but instead generally discuss skills and abilities of the individual. They will address qualities of the individual as an employee and can be used in a variety of job applications. A generic letter allows the applicant to submit a letter without having to ask their reference for a new letter for every position for which they are applying. If someone writes you a generic letter of recommendation, make sure to keep copies of the letter, both in print and electronic formats.

Is the letter for an application to another college or graduate school? These letters will discuss the academic abilities of the individual and how successful they are likely to be in an academic program.

As you might imagine, the format of these letters would be quite different.

Have a Letter Ready to Go

I have found that when I have asked for a reference letter, the person would often ask me to write a draft letter of reference that they could edit and use to create the official version. This is extremely common. When you're getting references from others, you should have some sort of basic letter drafted that you can offer them to use as a starting point. They can edit this letter to match what you are applying for. Make sure to tell them specifically what the letter is for so that they can tailor it for the application.

If there are specific requirements for the letter, make sure that those are covered and that you provide that information to your reference.

The draft should include information about how you know the person and what they would be able to recommend about you, such as strong customer service or technology skills.

There are certain categories of information that would be relevant in almost any letter, such as your technology or people skills and on the job experience.

Only include information about yourself that the person would know via direct contact. For example, I can't include information that I've heard from others about you. I can only include personal experiences that I've had with you.

The text of your letter should be about 1 page (at most) and include 1–2 paragraphs about yourself. Don't worry about formatting it as a letter. Your reference will take the text of the letter, edit it as needed, format it, print it on official letterhead, and sign it.

Don't Forget the Thank You

As a courtesy, if you make it through the application process and actually interview for a position, make sure to let your reference know what has happened with a phone call or email. This will alert them to prepare for a call they may receive about you within the next week or so.

And if you get the position or are accepted into that academic program, make sure to thank your reference. I love to hear when I played any sort of role in the success of another person.

Always check in with your references if you are applying for a job.

You need to make sure they are prepared when they get the call from your potential employer.

You need to make sure that they're still willing to give you a positive review.

You might want to consider contacting them at the beginning of the application process to let them know what you're up to.

If your supervisor likes you, they will give you a good review.

Even if the official company policy is to only supply dates of employment and other basic information, if your supervisor will find a way to give a good review of someone. They may do it on their own time and from their own phone.

Web Resources on Letters of Recommendation

The following are a few useful web resources on this topic:

• Sample Letters of Recommendation –
http://www.boxfreeconcepts.com/reco/sample.html

• Writing a Reference Letter (With Examples) –
http://www.dailywritingtips.com/writing–a–reference–letter–with–examples

• Top 10 Sample Recommendation Letters –
http://businessmajors.about.com/od/samplerecommendations/tp/TopRecLetters.htm

3.10 Thank You Notes

I've read a few discussions on job hunting websites about whether you should still send thank you notes.

I like thank you notes because they're a way of showing gratitude, connecting to others and strengthening bonds.

On a more practical level, they are another tool you can use in your professional life, particularly if you are looking for a job.

Why not send one? It can't hurt. In fact, it may help. I'm more likely to fondly remember an individual who's written me a thank you note.

There are a variety of situations, such as receiving a gift or attending a party, where sending a thank you note can make quite a nice impression.

In your professional life, thank you note can be even more important. You don't have to send a note for every interaction you have with every person, but think about when you might want to do this.

Here are a few questions to ask yourself to determine if you want to thank someone with a note:

- Are you looking for a job?
- Did they go out of their way to help you?
- Did they do something particularly nice for you?
- Did they connect you to others who might help you?
- Did they spend some of their valuable time working with you?
- Is this the first time you've worked with someone?
- Are they from another organization or company?
- Are they from another industry?
- Are they at a higher level than you?
- Are they well established in their career?
- Are you or they moving to something different? (job or location)

Email or Handwritten Note

Which option should you choose? I've seen some debate about whether to send handwritten thank you notes. Does it seem old fashioned? Does it do any good?

As with so many other things, it depends on the culture of the organization to which you are communicating. You would want to assess how "techie" the recipient of your note is and how tech heavy the organization is when you're deciding whether to send an email or a handwritten card. Evaluate the context and adjust accordingly. It also depends on the person you are communicating with. If you know that they hate to deal with paper, send an email rather than a note.

Personally, I really like it when I receive a handwritten thank you note. I've also heard this from others.

If you have really bad handwriting, you might want to email or print out a note.

If you are concerned with speed (you want it to get there really fast) and wanted to send something more quickly than snail mail, you could send a quick email to your recipient. I would however follow it up with a handwritten note.

Additionally, a handwritten note may indicate more than you think it does.

To me it represents the following:

• Going the extra mile (not everyone sends a thank you note so this is a way for you to stand out)
• A better understanding of professional etiquette which is a skill that many people seem to lack
• Attention to detail
• That you really want this job

Even if you don't get hired for this job, it will create a memory that you are above average and may have an impact on future hiring decisions.

It's like sowing a seed that may flower later.

Writing Your Note

No Errors Please. If you've interviewed well but then send a thank you note that is full of errors, you've undone any positive impression that you may have made.

Make sure you run spell check and grammar check before you send your email. In situations like this I don't fill in the To: field until I'm sure I want to send it. This avoids any accidental sends that may happen.

For any handwritten note, I compose the text on my computer and then copy it to the card. This allows me to avoid mistakes and send the exact message I want to send. Finally, make sure to choose nice stationary or cards to add to the good impression.

Thank You Note Examples

Here are a couple examples of a fairly standard thank you note format.

You'll notice that each note contains specifics relating to the interview and/or about the experience and qualifications of the writer.

Thank You Example Note 1:

Date:

Dear Pamela Posz,

Thank you very much for your time on Wednesday. I truly appreciate the opportunity to interview for the full-time position.

With my experience and background, I know I would immediately contribute to the librarian team during this time of transition.

I am excited to have the possible opportunity to work with the librarians to energize the library outreach initiatives and to continue to help our wonderful students succeed.

I look forward to hearing from you soon.

Thanks again,

Signature

Thank You Example Note 2

Date:

Dear Mr. Scott,

It was very enjoyable to speak with you about the maintenance position at Smithville Inc.. The job, as you presented it, seems to be a very good match for my skills and interests.

In addition to my enthusiasm, I will bring to the position a positive attitude and also will have the ability to encourage others to work cooperatively with the department. My background will help me to work with customers and staff and provide me with an understanding of the visual aspects of our work.

I understand your need for customer support. My detail orientation and organizational skills will help to free you to deal with larger issues.

I appreciate the time you took to interview me. I am very interested in working for you and look forward to hearing from you about this position.

Sincerely,

Signature

Chapter 4 – Interviewing

4.1 Interviewing Basics

This section will help you with all of your interview skills.

We'll discuss:

- How to dress for the interview
- Your Interview preparation schedule
- Interview preparation techniques and behavioral interviewing
- Don'ts (things to avoid)
- How to perform in the actual interview
- Stress reduction for interviewing
- And much more

Practice and Preparation

The key to interviewing well is preparation and practice. Every book that I looked at about interviewing will tell you to prepare and practice. This book is no exception. Over time I've had a few people suggest that you should just wing it if you want to interview well because you'll be able to improvise. That has not been my experience either personally when I've interviewed for jobs, or when I've interviewed others.

You can't control whether you get the job. You can only control how well you interview. If you're prepared – it's much more likely that you'll get the job.

Mentally prepare – Prepare for what you'll say.

Physically prepare – Prepare for how you'll dress. Figure out transportation. Make copies of your resume.

Prepare to de-stress on the day of the interview.

Prepare for the interview. Prepare for the interview. Prepare for the interview.

Practice your answers to standard questions out loud whenever possible.

You also might want to practice in front of someone who can give you some good constructive criticism.

Practice anything that you aren't comfortable with.

The more you practice, the more prepared you will be and hopefully you'll be somewhat less stressed out in a highly stressful environment.

4.2 How to Dress for an Interview

How to Dress

Research shows that it takes anywhere from 2 – 30 seconds to form a first impression of another person.[16] Your appearance is obviously extremely important for an interview and for any other professional interactions.

Your dress and grooming are key.

The following are recommendations rather than rules based on what I've observed in mock interviews.

If you want to try something different, particularly if it helps you feel confident, then you should do what you prefer.

Just make sure that your interview attire is formal enough.

Additionally, if you know that your field has different ideas about to dress for an interview than I have written here, go with what is appropriate for your field.

 Networking Strikes Again – How Should You Dress?

If you aren't sure, try to interview or get advice from someone in your field to give you some direction. "How should I dress during an interview?" would be an excellent question to ask during an informational interview.

Go for Formal

In general, your best option for an interview is formal business attire, such as a suit, or some version of a suit.

It makes you look professional. It shows that you understand business culture. It indicates attention to detail. You look like you are eager to get the job.

Personally, I like to wear a suit for a job interview. I know it looks good, I come across in a more professional manner and I don't really have make decisions about what I'll be wearing. This allows me to concentrate on the actual interview.

Even if you will be dressing casually once you start the job, you should dress up for the interview.

Strive for Neutral

A neutral look is important because you want the interviewer(s) to focus on what you're saying rather than your appearance.

For example, even if tattoos are ubiquitous in your industry, I would try to cover up any tattoos during an interview. You can't be certain that others won't have a negative reaction to your specific tattoos.

The same rule applies to piercings. You should take out any visible piercings, except for earrings. This includes nose, lip and tongue piercings. As with tattoos, they may be acceptable on the job. However, you don't know how people will react during the interview and you are striving for a neutral presentation.

If you know for certain that any or all tattoos or piercings are OK in your industry, feel free to ignore this advice. If you aren't certain, I would follow this advice.

Choose One Item of Clothing That's Unique

I know this may seem to be contradictory, given that I just said to be neutral. However, I do recommend wearing one item of clothing that stands out, such as a colorful waistcoat, an interesting tie, or a colorful blouse. This will help the interview committee remember you and help you feel attractive and confident. This brings me to...

Specific Interview Clothing Suggestions

Women's Interview Attire

- Solid color, conservative suit or business dress
- Coordinated blouse
- Moderate shoes
- Limited jewelry
- Neat, professional hairstyle
- Tan or light hosiery
- Sparse make-up & no perfume or scent
- Manicured nails
- Portfolio or briefcase

Mind the Gap (Your Cleavage)

Mind the gap – i.e. watch your cleavage. Choose tops with a high neckline. If you have a neckline that isn't high, bend over in front of a mirror, hunch your shoulders forward to see if there is any sort of cleavage showing. If you see any cleavage, you need to choose a different outfit or wear something like a half camisole under the shirt.

Men's Interview Attire

- Solid color, conservative suit
- White long sleeve shirt
- Conservative tie
- Dark socks, professional shoes
- Very limited jewelry
- Neat, professional hairstyle
- No aftershave or fragrance
- Neatly trimmed nails
- Portfolio or briefcase

Check Yourself So You Don't Wreck Yourself

If you are wearing pants, always check your fly before you meet anyone at the interview site.

Perhaps a Suit?

The higher level the position, the closer you should get to wearing a suit.

If you can't afford a suit, borrow one that fits well enough. If you really can't get a decent suit, purchase a jacket and wear it with a tie.

A pair of slacks and a long–sleeved dress shirt with a tie is a nice option that's slightly less formal.

As always, if you have inside information (i.e. you know someone who works for the organization and they indicate that you shouldn't wear a suit, listen to the insider). However, if you have no inside information, always go more formal and suit up.

Can't Afford Interview Clothes?

If you can't afford professional clothes for an interview, you might want to check with local charities. For example, homeless shelters often have special collections of professional clothing for job seekers. You can also find excellent options for very little money at a used clothing store.

Feel Confident

Above all else you need to find something to wear that makes you feel confident.

Although you should select clothes that are more formal, do not choose anything that makes you physically uncomfortable.

If you never wear clothes that are formal but need to wear a more formal interview outfit, practice wearing your clothes before the interview.

If you need help selecting an interview outfit, try asking the salesperson at the store for help. Several of my students have had good luck working with someone in the suit section at a well-known department store chain. There wasn't any pressure to buy more expensive items, they truly helped them find an appropriate outfit. This can be particularly useful when you are interviewing for professional positions.

Even if the workplace is casual, you should still dress formally for the interview.

Make sure to read the earlier section on interpersonal and networking skills such as body language. These are equally as important as your clothes during an interview.

4.3 Interview Preparation Schedule

If you are working with any sort of technology such as in a Skype interview, you'll need to give yourself a little more lead time to make sure everything works correctly and to come up with backup options. Check out section 4.13 for specific tips if you have a distance interview with a phone call or video interviews.

For example, if possible, print out any documents ahead of time that you might need to bring on the interview. If you don't have a printer, make screen shots you can access even if your phone can't connect to the network. Or copy out the directions by hand on to a piece of paper that you can carry with you. I love using paper as a backup because it's pretty full proof. My phone has been known to fail me in the past. I don't want this to happen on the day of the interview.

I will also usually try to visit the interview location ahead of time to ensure I know where I'm going, and to see what the parking situation is like. If possible, I try to do a dry run at the same time of day as the interview so that I'm aware of traffic patterns that may slow me down. You can also use Google maps and other mapping software to estimate how long a drive will be at a specific time of day.

Practice Your Timing

Time yourself answering potential interview questions (such as those in this book) and see how long it takes for you to answer the question. You can practice until the time falls in the right range.

If you prepare ahead of time, you can focus on relaxing and mentally preparing yourself for the interview and you'll do better.

If possible, try to take the day off or time off the day of your interview. You'll be more relaxed and it will allow you to better manage your time.

Right before your interview watch or read or listen to something funny. It will relax you and you should do better in the interview.

Read your resume before you go into the interview.

Remember to be nice to everyone you meet whenever you visit the organization, particularly on the day of the interview. You don't know who everyone is. Any of the people you talk to could have some influence on the interview. Even if an individual isn't on your interview current panel, you may have to work with them if you get the job. Or they may be involved in future hiring decisions. If you interview with an organization more than one time that individual could be on your panel the next time. Be nice to everyone you meet.

In some cases, how you treat a person may be part of the interview process.

If you are submitting a lot of applications and you expect that you might be interviewed, you should be prepared for an interview at any time. This is another area where networking can be useful. If you know of someone within the organization, they can give you an idea about how much time the process may take and what you might expect from the process.

This is a suggested schedule of logistical preparations and activities you can use to prepare for your interview.

Adjust this schedule according to how much time you've been given up until the interview. Don't panic if you aren't able to do everything on this list, these are suggested activities you can do to prepare. Any of these should help prepare you for the interview.

Written Interview Preparation

Your most important preparations for an interview should be preparing for how you'll answer potential questions. I'll cover that in sections 4.4 and 4.5, Written Interview Preparation.

Once you've created all of your potential answers, there are a few things you should practice.

Practice your elevator speech out loud whenever possible.

I often do it in my car as I'm driving around.

Time yourself talking for 3 minutes to get a sense of how long that is. It's a nice amount of time to talk in an interview. Since your sense of time will be off because you're under stress, it's good to get a feel for this ahead of time.

Memorize your stories.

The rest of this section will provide you with a schedule for the logistical details for preparing for the interview.

You've Been Notified that You'll be Interviewing

Your application has made it through the screening process and you've been notified you'll be interviewing.

Pick Your Time Slot

If possible, try to choose the earliest or latest time slots. The earliest slots are preferable because the panel sees you when they are fresh in the morning and haven't been listening to everyone interview all day. The later slots are preferable because it is more likely that the members of the panel will remember the final few candidates.

You may have time to review the questions before the interview begins. Many organizations will give you approximately 10 minutes to review the questions and make notes.

The worst interview time slot is right after lunch. Your panel may be sleepy and find it hard to concentrate. You will also be in the middle.

If you have one or more weeks to prepare.

If the interview is several weeks away, here are a few things you might want to do in order to prepare.

If possible, take the day off work, or at least an hour or two of time before the interview.

If you have to travel to an interview, you obviously will have to take the time off work to travel and interview.

However, even if you are interviewing locally, if possible, I'd suggest taking the time off work on the day of the interview.

This will reduce your amount of stress. You might be able to avoid bad traffic. No one will give you any last-minute projects. You'll have all of the time you need to get dressed and ready. Obviously, not everyone will be able to do this. Some people won't be able to get the extra time away from work.

Week Before the Interview

Get Your Interview Outfit Together

Try on your outfit to ensure it looks good and is appropriate for the interview. You need to allow yourself enough time to purchase a new interview outfit if necessary.

Practice Your Timing

Time yourself answering potential interview questions (such as those in this book) and see how long it takes for you to answer the question. You can practice until the time falls in the right range.

Visit the Interview Location

Obviously, this isn't possible for everyone. If you're flying in for an interview, you won't be able to visit ahead of time. However, if you can visit ahead of time, and you haven't already scouted it out during your interview preparation, try to visit before the interview. It's particularly useful to do this at the same time of day in which you'll be interviewing as it will give you a sense of what the traffic will be like. You'll also be able to see where you can park and find what building you'll be in. Knowing all of this ahead of time means you won't be trying to figure out where everything is located at the last minute and is another way to reduce your stress on the day of the interview.

Figure Out Traffic and Parking

If you can't visit the interview location at the same time you would be interviewing, you can use Google or other traffic apps to figure out when you should leave. Make sure that you plan on arriving at least 10 minutes early and add an additional cushion of time in case there's a problem.

You might want to consider taking Lyft to the interview if parking is difficult. The lower stress level will be worth it.

Week of the Interview

Practice your opening speech in your car, at home, to friends and family members or anyone else who will listen.

Print out anything that you want to take with you to the interview such as copies of your resume.

Put the phone number for the interview contact in your phone. If something happens on the day of the interview, you need to be able to contact them.

Print out directions to the interview or at least make a screen shot. Don't save this for the night before. What if your printer runs out of ink or fails? Remember that technology can always fail.

Print out any other documents you need, resumes, work samples. Anything you might need during the interview.

Make sure that if you are doing a presentation or have any online materials that you will display during the interview, that you clear your computer of anything embarrassing or distracting that might show up if others see your technology. It will also make your materials easier to find when you are in the stressful situation of the interview. Either clear out a USB stick that you already own, buy a new USB stick that only has your materials on it. If you have materials in the cloud, make sure to create a separate clear folder that is easy to access at a top level.

Find a folder for any printed documents. I like to get something that looks nice for the interview.

Prepare any other backup versions you might need for the interview such as a USB stick with your documents, or screen shots on your phone.

Load up anything you might want to access online. Check it from more than one computer to make sure it works.

Clear out your technology backups (such as USB sticks or online drives) so that any interview materials are easily found and non-interview and personal material is hidden in folders with innocuous file names.

You might want to get a USB stick that you only use for interviews. You do not want weird personal folder names or folders with other places where you are interviewing to be visible during your interview. If you are using your laptop – clean up your desktop and just have 1 folder visible for the interview. This will also make it easier to find your interview materials when you are stressed out during the interview.

Pack the materials you'll need during the interview. These include pen or pencil, a pad of paper, a copy of your resume and any other materials you've been instructed to bring such as letters of reference.

Always bring copies of your resume for an interview. Ask how many people will be on the committee and add an extra copy or two just in case. Don't assume that everyone on the panel has seen your resume.

Gather Your Interview Supplies

These are what you should have during the interview:

- Copies of resume
- Work portfolio
- Pad of Paper
- Pens/Pencils
- If possible, print versions of anything electronic you are demonstrating
- Backup versions of any electronic materials you are bringing

Your Emergency Kit

These are items you might want to keep in your car or bag when you go to interview. These will cover most "emergencies" that you can easily handle.

To Carry with You

- A snack (particularly for all day interviews)
- Water bottle
- Cash
- Tylenol/aspirin, antacids, eye drops, Band-Aids
- Dental floss
- Comb and brush
- Deodorant
- Phone charging supplies: cord, battery, wall plug
- Lint roller
- Sharpie – for coloring stains or snags
- Clear nail polish and/or superglue – to repair snags
- Safety pins
- An instant stain remover like one of the Tide pens
- Breath mints or chewing gum. The breath mints or gum are particularly important. If you're stressed out and your adrenaline spikes, your mouth will dry out. Suck on a breath mint to get your saliva going so that you can speak. Chewing gum can also reduce stress. Just remember to spit out the gum before the interview.

Leave in the Car

- An extra shirt for massive spills
- A change of shoes in case you have to walk a lot
- Extra contact lenses
- Umbrella
- Extra panty–hose or tights
- Pad or tampon
- Makeup and hair products
- An extra neck–tie

Bring a Briefcase

If you are wondering how you'll tote around all of this stuff, you should have an attractive bag that can function as your briefcase where you can store all of your supplies. You may want to pack smaller items in a small bag to contain and organize them within the larger bag. Personally, I love pencil pouches for this purpose.

Make sure that it is organized so that you'll be able to access what you need in your briefcase without a lot of "digging" around. If you have made a good impression and your bag spills, or you can't find what you need in it, that good impression may disappear.

Day Before the Interview

Take care of last-minute preparations to avoid dealing with them on the day of your interview:

Fill up your tank with gas. It'll add unnecessary time to your schedule and you don't want your hands to smell of gasoline.

Lay out your interview outfit.

Plan your schedule for the day of the interview.

Most importantly get a good night's sleep. Sleep is probably the most important thing you can do to have a good day when you interview.

Day of the Interview

Eat a good breakfast

Review your resume one last time.

If you smoke, finish your last cigarette with enough time so that you don't smell of cigarette smoke for the interview.

Because you've prepared for the interview ahead of time it should be a fairly stress-free morning.

Use the strategies in section 4.7 (Interviewing and Stress Reduction) to further calm yourself before the interview.

Right Before the Interview

You should plan to arrive about 10–15 minutes before the interview. No more. No less.

Before you check in, use the techniques to reduce your stress level, particularly the breathing exercises that are covered in section 4.7. Mentally prepare for the moment you walk into the interview room. You've prepared really well so you'll do great.

If you've been chewing gum, spit it out.

Run your hands under hot water before the interview so that you don't have cold/clammy hands. Your hands will be less sweaty.

Turn off your cell phone completely when you arrive.

The Power Posz

Dr. Amy Cuddy, a social psychologist, has found in her research that standing in a "Power Pose" (a.k.a. like a superhero) can have a really positive impact on confidence levels and can lower stress levels thereby improving your performance in stressful situations, such as job interviews.

I'd recommend watching her 2012 TED talk on the subject – "Your body language may shape who you are."[17]

This seemed like such good advice for my students that I introduced them to it starting in 2012. They, in turn started to use it in their own lives and reported positive results when, for example, they tried the power pose before an interview. It wasn't long before they renamed it as the Power Posz, which is what they all call it now, and how this book came by its title.

Try it out at home and see how you feel.

If you follow any portion of these suggestions, you should be completely prepared and have a great interview.

4.4 Written Interview Preparation – STAR

Interview Questions

You'll find a list of interview questions that I've collected in the appendix at the back of this book.

It's a fairly extensive list and covers common categories that you might encounter in a typical interview.

However, for any interview, you should also be prepared for questions that are specific to your field. For example, what are the questions you might expect if you're a librarian or a zoologist or a psychologist. Fortunately, there's an excellent website you can explore that will help you with these questions. It's called MockQuestions (https://www.mockquestions.com). You can use this site to search for interview questions for many jobs and this site will provide you a common set of questions. More importantly, MockQuestions provides suggestions for high quality answers that you can use in an interview. It's a pretty amazing resource.

Master Interview Document

Once you have identified a job that you'll apply for and you have analyzed the job ad (see section 1.5) you should start to prepare for an interview.

Your best option is to create a master document that you can easily access and edit (mine is a Google doc).

By creating it in writing, you won't have to recreate your answers every time you interview. You'll just need to study your document before the interview to refresh your memory.

Your answers will also have better flow if you write them out and include more detail, i.e. write stories.

This master document will save you quite a bit of time and you can continue to update it as you progress in your career.

The Short Version

Once you've created the long version, create a shorter outline version that you can take with you to interviews.

What's in this document?

You will take the list of categories you have identified in the job announcement and write out stories based on your work history that demonstrate how your experience matches the job requirements.

For example, if the job lists customer service, technology, communication, critical thinking, and diversity and inclusion; you should have stories for each of these categories.

Most of the stories should have a specific structure known as the STAR technique. It is used in Behavioral Interviewing.

What Is Behavioral Interviewing?

If you haven't heard about behavioral interviewing, don't worry. It's unfamiliar to many people, although it is commonly used in the private sector.

Behavioral interviewing is different than traditional interviewing. The concept behind it is that past performance is the best predictor of future performance.

The questions are structured differently from traditional interview questions. Instead of asking a somewhat generic question such as "What is your experience working with people?" the question would be "Please describe a situation where you had to assist a difficult patron."

Many of the questions start with "tell us about a time when...." or "give me an example of a time when you..."

In a true behavioral interview, there would be a series of follow up questions to really delve into your performance in that situation.

Although behavioral interviewing is not typically used in the public sector, it's been my experience that if you answer traditional interview questions in a behavioral style, your answers will be very strong and you will do well in the interview.

Additionally, they make it more likely that you'll give answers that fully respond to the question rather than 1 word or sentence answers that sometimes emerge when an interviewee is extremely nervous.

Master List of Behavioral Interview Questions

You can simply Google this topic and you will, of course, find millions of options.

One that I'd recommend is the "Complete List of Behavioral Interview Questions," by Alex Rudloff.[18] It's a well-organized and extensive list of these types of questions. You'll notice that many of them begin with "Tell us about a time that...." Or "Describe a time when you...."

The STAR Technique

The true foundation to behavioral interviewing is the STAR technique. It's a technique you can use to structure your answers for maximum effect.

Not every story has to match the STAR technique, but it's worth giving it a try because it's really effective.

If possible, each story you record should describe the general situation, describe a task or responsibility you had to complete, the action you took, and the result or your work.

Situation

Task

Action

Result

STAR Example

I was working in a school library at Elena Nguyen Elementary School and the school budget included hardly any money that could be used to purchase new books for the library.

I decided to organize a Scholastic book sale in order to increase the amount of money for the library budget. There were a number of steps I had to take to make this a successful project.

I got permission from the principle, I contacted scholastic, found volunteers to assist me, trained the volunteers, created advertising materials for the fair, maintained inventory throughout the fair.

The fair was extremely successful and I raised over $3,000 for the library budget. We were able to add 250 new items to the collection and save the remaining $1000 for the following year.

Several teachers have already agreed to help out next year and the principle stopped to personally congratulate me. It was a very successful activity and I will be repeating it again next year.

How does that compare to "I ran a book sale at my school" as an answer?

Takeaways

There are a few things I'd like to highlight about this story and how it would work in an interview.

Stories are a really effective and memorable way to convey information. People remember stories much more than most other types of information.

You should develop stories that can be used for multiple categories.

One of the benefits of doing a lot of interview preparation, particularly behavioral interview preparation is that you'll be able to develop stories that you can use in multiple categories. This will allow you to avoid repeating the same story in more than one question. I could use the story in this example for many different categories such as outreach, financial skills, pro–activity, teamwork, marketing, and more. I'd just need to tweak it slightly depending on what I wanted to emphasize.

The details make stories more memorable. Include detail whenever possible with all of your job-hunting materials, from the application to your resume, to the interview.

The numbers in this story make it more memorable.

Always include numbers in your stories whenever they make sense and add detail.

Preparation is key for a good interview and is required if you're going to do behavioral style interview techniques. It is unlikely that I would have used a story with this level of detail if I hadn't prepared it ahead of time.

4.5 Written Interview Preparation – Beyond STAR

Other than the categories you identify in the job announcement, here are the STAR stories you should create ahead of time.

What are Your 5 Things?

With all of your materials and preparation you should try to figure out 3–5 things about yourself that you want to convey. These are sort of like your elevator speech.

You should include them in your application materials and interview answers.

These traits may also help you identify stories and examples you want to use in your STAR preparation.

For example, my 5 things are creativity, love diverse working environments, love helping people, technology skills, teaching skills. I try to include at least one of these characteristics in each of the stories I've recorded.

The following are common traits that might be your "5 things":

- People skills
- Teamwork
- Technology skills
- Time Management
- Attention to Detail
- Management
- Communication
- Creativity
- Pro–activity

- Diversity
- Problem solver
- Reliable
- Flexible – adaptable
- Enthusiasm
- Adaptability
- Commitment to Professional Development

TUALBAY – Tell Us A Little Bit About Yourself

I have never participated in an interview, either as an interviewer or as the interviewee where some version of this question is not the first question.

I would guarantee that you'll get this question in every job interview (with the exception of a really informal interview).

What's the key to answering it?

You should give a short summary of your work history while relating it to the current position. You should also convey how much you want to work for this specific organization.

And remember to convey those 5 things.

You can't control any of the other interview questions. This is the one you have the most control over. You get to tell your story.

I Taught Chess to Children or What's Memorable About You?

You should have one unique and memorable story that also fits one of the categories you identified in the job ad. Remember that the interviewers or interview panel is probably trapped in a room for 1 or more days that has no natural light. Even with the best of intentions and the best note taking skills, candidates start to blur together. You should have one story that has something unique in your interview preparation. This will give the interviewers something to remember you by and you'll hopefully stand out from the pack.

Examples: taught chess to children, owned own hair salon, taught archery at Renaissance festivals, worked in the cheese department at Whole Foods, worked at the Library of Congress.

Equity, Diversity, and Anti-Racism

Particularly with the public sector, it is extremely likely that you will need to address diversity in your application materials and the job interview.

Employers are generally trying to decide how comfortable you are working in a diverse environment and if applicable, helping a diverse group of clients.

Here is an example of a typical diversity question: "Please describe examples of when you have worked successfully with diverse customers/clients and staff and explain how you would use any such related skills on the job."

Although people often think of diversity simply in terms of race, it is important to realize that it's a much broader concept. Race is one aspect of it, but diversity covers a wide variety of different issues. Here are a few examples of different types of diversity:

- Race
- Socioeconomic status
- Learning disabilities
- Physical disabilities
- Mental health
- LGBTQIAA+
- Age
- Cultural differences and the ability to work well with those who are from other countries
- Technological abilities and access to technology

 Networking Strikes Again – Knowing the Organization

This is another area where knowing the organization and networking can be useful. If you know someone in that type of position, or even better at the organization, you'll have a better idea about how to answer a diversity question because you'll know what the work environment will be. You'll be able to tailor your application and interview questions to cover this. For example, if you were applying to an organization that assists homeless gay teens, even if the diversity question was somewhat generic, you'd want to emphasize your experience with LGBTQIAA+ issues in your application and interview.

One final thing about diversity. Although you may be a member of one of the groups listed above, make sure to do more than simply state that you are part of that group. You'll still need to address your ability to work in a diverse setting.

Strengths and Weaknesses

One of the most common interview questions that you may encounter is "What is your greatest strength?" It is often combined with "What is your greatest weakness?" Anyone who is going for an interview should have answers prepared for both of these questions.

Most people have some idea about how they should answer the strength question because they are happy to discuss a talent or skill they have but struggle with how to describe a weakness in a manner that is honest, but not negative.

There are a few strategies you can use to come up with answers to these questions.

One way to think about this is that strengths are generally things that you enjoy doing or that you are good at.

Here are a few examples:

• One of my strengths is that I'm creative and am happiest when I'm creating things
• I love to help people
• I have strong technology skills

As with all of your interview answers, you should try to answer these questions with concrete examples rather than general answers that don't really mean anything.

I've listed generic statements. If this were an interview, I would follow them with concrete examples that support the first statement.

Most people would consider the weakness question is the harder one to answer. However, a strategy I've found for discussing your weakness is that weaknesses are often things that we struggle with or don't feel we're particularly good at.

There are a few considerations to keep in mind when coming up with a weakness.

Don't choose something that is really negative and would mean that someone wouldn't want to hire you. For example, don't mention anything that indicates that you don't like to work with people. No employer wants an employee who can't work with others.

I would not use either: being a perfectionist or working too hard as your weakness. Both are problematic in different ways.

Choose something that is true, don't make something up.

Once you decide what you'll talk about, you then need to talk about how you compensate for your weakness.

If you can include technology in your answer about how you compensate for your weakness, that is a bonus.

Read It Aloud

Once you've written out your master interviewing document, I'd suggest you read some or all of the answers aloud, particularly the tell us a little bit about yourself section. You'll catch errors you may have made. Things sound different when you read them aloud.

4.6 Don'ts – The Bad and the Ugly

These issues may be obvious to some of you; however, I've heard enough stories of these behaviors happening in interviews that I wanted to lay them out in this section.

They are all behaviors you need to absolutely avoid during any interviews or professional interactions.

Things to Avoid

Appearance
- Poor grooming, appearance, and clothing choices
- Wearing sunglasses (even on the top of your head)
- Chewing gum
- Cross your arms. It's bad non–verbal communication.

Behavior
- Smoking
- Drinking or Eating
- Personal grooming such as combing hair, brushing teeth, or picking your nose, picking your face.
- Wearing a fragrance – the interview panel might not like the scent you've chosen or could even be allergic to scents.
- Jokes – although you should be pleasant. You do not want to tell a joke that offends anyone.
- Being rude to anyone at the organization. You don't know who anyone is. What if interacting with the assistant is a test to see whether you're a pleasant person? Be really nice to everyone you meet.
- Leaving your cell phone on or answer it during an interview. Turn it off completely and put it away. It will distract you if it's out.
- Try to avoid saying the word "no" in your answers. It leaves a negative impression.
- Don't ask the panel what they are looking for in a candidate. That information is listed in the job description.

Never, Ever, Ever

• Make inappropriate comments or jokes.

• Act like you're too good or overqualified for the position.

• Mentioning the wrong employer. For example, you mention Google and the job is at Facebook.

• Badmouth a current or previous employer.

• Tell the interviewer that you lied to come to the interview today.

• Answer your cell phone during an interview. You should be able to completely turn off your phone during an interview. If for some reason (the only one that comes to mind is that your wife is pregnant and may go into labor at any minute) get the number of the assistant who has been your contact at the potential employer and give that to your wife in case of emergency.

• Never indicate in any way that you don't like to work with other people. This could include working with children, with the elderly or any other specific group.

• Never offer criticism of the potential employer. For example, "Your website is really bad, I'd love to improve it." The interview is not the place to make these suggestions. You may alienate someone on the panel. What if you criticize work that's been done by one of the members of your interview panel?

• Never ask about salary or benefits during the interview. Save these discussions for after you've received a job offer.

• Never ask about others who may be interviewing or how many other candidates are to be interviewed.

• Don't ask questions that could easily be answered by looking at the company website. You should
have already done this sort of research when you were preparing for the interview.

Based the on many discussions of job hunting I've had with all sorts of different people; the job interview is definitely the most stressful part of the entire process. There are a variety of reasons for this.

There's a huge fear of failure. You really want that job!

The physical layout of an interview is unlikely to put you at your ease. You often have to sit across a table from one or more people while you wear business attire, which is generally not the most comfortable clothing we own.

It's very normal to be nervous during your interview. Almost everyone is nervous for job interviews (there are a few strange people who aren't but they're the anomalies). The people interviewing you will expect you to be nervous. Some nervousness can even be good as it comes across as energetic. The key is to control your nervousness so that it doesn't incapacitate you.

This section of the book will give you strategies to help you manage your stress, avoid choking, and improve how well you interview.

That's Not a Lion Chasing You

Before we go into the stress reduction strategies I have for you, let's discuss what's going on with all of the stress that's likely to happen, particularly during an interview. If you understand why you're stressed out and how it's affecting your body, you should be able to manage it better and improve your interview skills.

Bear with me. We're going back in time. A very long time...

Human beings evolved over millions and millions of years to avoid being eaten by a variety of different predators that thought we were delicious and nutritious. We either had to try to fight the lion or run away from the lion, commonly referred to as the fight or flight response. It's really useful on the Serengeti. Unfortunately, it also kicks in during interviews and other stressful situations.

This means that your body doesn't realize that you are interviewing for a job. It thinks you are running away from a lion...or tiger...or bear and triggers a set of physiological responses that make it more likely that you'll survive. The sweaty palms and increased heart rate are part of this.

And most importantly, your brain also doesn't work the same way when you're stressed. This means you may not be at your mental best, particularly if you are super stressed.

Conversely, if you can reduce your stress level, you will do better in job interviews.

Stress Reduction Strategies

Here are a few strategies and techniques you can use to reduce stress before the interview.

166

Slow Your Breathing

This is definitely the most important activity you can do to reduce stress.

When you are stressed out part of the physiological response is that your breathing changes. It becomes more rapid and shallow.

However, if you can slow your breathing down, you can actually trick your brain into relaxing your body and reducing your stress.

Here's an easy technique you can use to slow down your breathing. Make sure to practice this technique ahead of time so you know what it feels like and can use it right before the interview to relax.

Find a comfortable place to sit.

Close your eyes and take a deep breath in for 4–5 counts. If you place your hand on your stomach, it should move. These are deep breaths.

Hold the breath in for another 4–5 counts

Let it out softly and slowly for another 4–5 counts. Visualize a lit candle. Let your breath out slowly so that the candle doesn't go out.

Repeat the exercise several times and it should calm you down and relax you a bit. You could do this a few times in your car once you've arrived at the interview location. You would probably want to keep your eyes open if you're sitting in a visible spot, waiting for the interview.

If you want to look for other techniques, I'd recommend searching for "calm breathing" in your search engine of choice.

Music

Listen to music that energizes you and improves your mood on the way to the interview. Play songs in the car while you're driving there. I would recommend songs that you enjoy singing along with. Your goal is to feel happy and confident by the time you arrive.

Walking on Sunshine by Katrina and the Waves is they type of music I'm talking about, but choose whatever makes you happy.

Walk Around

You should plan on arriving to the interview about 10–15 minutes early. If you arrive before that, or you could even schedule in an extra 10 minutes into your pre–interview schedule to do this, take the time to go for a little walk. Obviously, this won't always be possible. The weather and physical environment may not allow for it. However, walking around listening to music will work better than sitting in your car trying to mentally prepare yourself.

Look at Photos or Videos of Animals or Your Loved Ones

Research has proved that petting animals serves as a stress release. Blood pressure drops and people relax around animals.

More recent research has demonstrated that looking at pictures of animals can have almost the same effect. I have found that pictures of baby animals are the most effective. For many people, photos of their loved ones, such as their children, could also have a similar effect. You can either watch cat videos[19] or look at photos of baby animals.[20]

Watch a Funny Video

An alternative to baby animals is watching something amusing online. Nothing that will make you "lose it" where you're crying laughing. But something mildly funny that will make you smile.

Chew Gum

Chewing gum has been shown to reduce stress. Chew gum on the way to the interview, just remember to dispose of it before you walk into the building.

Talk to Yourself in the 2nd or 3rd Person

I was listening to an episode of the Hidden Brain podcast "Why It's Not Too Late to Make a New Year's Resolution"[21] and they mentioned some fascinating research that seemed appropriate for interviewees. If you are in a stressful situation such as a job interview, try to talk to yourself in the 2nd or 3rd person rather than the 1st person. For example, instead of saying to myself "Why am I so stressed out and worried?" I might say "Why is Pam worried about how she'll do? She's really well prepared and will do great!" Talking to yourself as if you are someone else, rather than with "I" statements, apparently reduces stress. "When people used second- or third-person self–talk (for example "Why does Kayla feel this way?") they reported feeling less anxious and actually performed better in challenging situations."

Another option in terms of self–talk is to tell yourself "I'm excited." I can talk myself out of something like "you've got this" and easily convince myself that I don't. But "I'm excited" just makes me happy and confident, the state of mind I'm aiming for in an interview.

Be Prepared

Know where you're going. Get everything ready the night before. Give yourself plenty of time. I've talked about specifics in previous sections. If you are unprepared and rushed that will increase your stress level. If you take care of everything ahead of time and are prepared it will allow you to focus on the interview and you will do better.

One way in which you can be prepared and that this book will set you up for is knowing which interview questions to expect. A big chunk of Chapter 4 deals with how to prepare to answer these questions. The Appendix also has an extensive list of interview questions. If you follow most of the instructions in this book, you should be really well prepared for your interview and your stress should drop somewhat.

Get Rid of Those Negative Thoughts

Write down negative thoughts and throw them away. A study has shown that you will be less affected by negative thoughts if you simply throw them away.[22]

4.8 The Actual Interview

Smile and Make Eye Contact

The two most important things you can do in an interview are to smile and make eye contact.

Because interviews are often a way for employers to see if you're a good fit and will work well with others, smiling is extremely important during an interview. However, this can be difficult in a situation where you're nervous, something that is almost guaranteed to happen during a job interview.

As with everything else, you might want to practice in front of a mirror to see how you look. For a natural smile, try to think of something positive such as a pet, friend, or loved one.

Here are a couple of suggestions for those who have a hard time making eye contact.

There are videos on YouTube where you can practice making eye contact.

Looking at the nose or forehead of the person you are talking with makes appear as if you are looking them in the eye. Try this with your friends if you don't think it's true.

 Networking Strikes Again – Interviewing

The actual interview is another situation where networking can be useful. If you know someone who is already working in the field in which you are interviewing, you should talk to them about what you might expect from a job interview.

If you know someone who actually works at that organization this is even more useful if they are able and willing to share the information. You can ask them about what you might expect in the interview. Will there be a writing sample? How many people are likely to be on the interview panel? How long will the interview take?

Make a Phone Call If You're Going to Be Late or Can't Make It

Legitimate emergencies do occasionally come up which will prevent you from being on time. Call if you encounter difficulties making it to the interview. They may be able to work with you and either wait or move you into another slot.

If this isn't possible, that's unfortunate. You will need to thank them for their time.

You should also call if you can't make it to the interview because something has come up or because you've decided not to interview.

In either case, communicate with your interview contact and thank them for their time.

With both of these scenarios, you can still lay groundwork or destroy the potential for future opportunities depending on your behavior.

If you are late and haven't let the panel know or if you simply don't show up this leaves a really poor impression.

But if you communicate professionally, you have left the door open.

In either case, make sure to have the phone number of your contact for the interview for emergency purposes.

Turn the Cell Phone Off – All the Way Off

I've mentioned this before, but it bears repeating. Don't leave your cell phone on or answer it during an interview. Turn it off completely and put it away. It will distract you if it's out.

If for some reason (the only one that comes to mind is that your wife is pregnant and may go into labor at any minute) you need to maintain contact with the outside world during the interview, get the number of the secretary and give that to your wife in case of emergency.

Use This Trick to Avoid Sweaty Palms and Fidgeting With Your Hands

This is a great trick to help with sweaty palms. Practice this before the interview.

Take your right hand and cup it like you're holding a tennis ball. It must be your right because that's the hand you shake with.

Your fingers should have a little space between them.

Place this hand palm down in your lap.

Then place your left hand over your right.

Because your right hand has some air flow it shouldn't become as sweaty as it would if you hold your hands together. Additionally, if you hold your hands in this position during the interview, you will avoid fidgeting with your hands, as well as any other equally distracting nervous habits such as playing with your hair or gesticulating too much.

How to Enter the Room

How you enter the room and sit down is the first impression the interviewers will have of you. There's a lot of research that indicates you make your first impression in the first minute you meet someone new.

Important Tip: if you are wearing pants, check your fly before you enter the room.

Walk in confidently, make eye contact and smile at everyone.

Wait until someone tells you where to sit in order to sit down.

Once you know where you're sitting, put your belongings down carefully, and sit down. Pull out anything you need for the interview (such as pen and paper) and place them in front of you. Take your time with this, but don't worry if everything doesn't exactly line up. You will not make a good first impression if you slump into the chair or throw any bags down into another chair or on the floor. On the

172

other end, if you take too much time lining up paper and pencil, people will read that as inflexibility. Go for a happy medium.

Ask if you can take notes. This can be useful if you need to clarify a question.

Ask if you can hand out your resume at the beginning of the interview. Then people can refer to it if they need to during an interview.

See section 4.11 to know how to deal with an interview when you already know someone on the panel.

Body Language and Other Physical Characteristics

Smile, smile, smile, smile, and then maybe smile. I can't emphasize this enough. If you're really nervous – try to think of something that makes you happy such as your dog or cat. Smiling will also make you feel happier and more confident. Additionally, there's research indicating that people who smile are viewed as being more intelligent.

Make eye contact. If it is an interview panel, make sure to make contact with everyone on the panel at some point during the interview.

Sit with your feet on the floor and your hands in your lap. Don't fidget. See the earlier section for a way to avoid this.

Use good posture, sit up straight and lean forward slightly.

Keep your body language open – avoid crossing your arms.

Look interested (i.e. make eye contact with anyone who's talking), and nod your head.

If you have to give a presentation or stand for any period of time, try to turn your hands so that your palms are facing the room. This is more welcoming body language.

Make sure you are loud enough so that everyone can hear you.

Water

The interviewer(s) will probably offer you water to drink during the interview. Unless your mouth is really dry and you can't speak or you are coughing, I would not drink the water until the end of the interview. It can be distracting if you drink during the interview particularly if the water is in a plastic bottle. That crinkly noise can be EXTREMELY distracting. Try squeezing a water bottle and see how much noise it makes.

They will provide you with water. Take a sip if your mouth is dry. Don't crinkle the bottle – it's really distracting.

If you really need to take a sip, time it so that you're drinking while a question is being asked.

Avoiding the Umms

Umms are what we do when our brain hasn't yet caught up to our mouths. They are verbal filler.

Everyone does it. The key is to avoid it for an actual interview as much as possible.

If you slow down your speech a little bit, you won't umm as much. Because you will be nervous and probably talking more quickly than normal, it is unlikely that you will sound too slow. This also has the side benefit of simply slowing down your speech a bit and you are more likely to sound normal.

Answering the Questions

Use complete sentences rather than yes or no.

Use behavioral interview techniques mentioned in section 4.4. This will help you to support your answers with examples and stories from your work history.

Be prepared to explain any gaps in your resume.

Use "I" not "We" where appropriate. If you were truly responsible for a project then your answers should reflect this.

Use positive language when describing your abilities and experience.

"I'm passionate about ...."

"I like to learn..."

"I enjoy working in a diverse environment"

Avoid asking or answering questions about your salary preferences.

If you dig yourself a hole, just stop digging. Don't keep talking if you have messed up. You can tell when this happens because the body language of the interviewers will change and they may stop recording and writing notes.

Don't just answer yes or no.

Never start any of your answers with a negative statement even if you don't have experience with what they are asking or you don't have those specific skills.

Never start with "I don't know how to do ...." or "I don't know." Even if they specifically ask if you know how to do something. Don't start with a No because the interview panel won't listen as well.

Instead, start with parallel or similar skills and after you've discussed what you know sufficiently, then at the end you can say that you don't actually have those skills.

Good Themes

There are a few general themes you can add to any answer you provide. These would also be good to emphasize in the 1st or last question.

Don't worry about using all of these. Pick one or two to integrate into your interview answers.

• You're easy to work with and enjoy working with people.
• You learn quickly.
• You aren't afraid to ask questions.

- You're proactive.
- You strive for excellence in everything you do.
- You like to say yes but you know when to say no.
- You're creative.

Handling Your Nervousness

Remember to do the stress reduction techniques I mentioned in section 4.7, particularly the breathing techniques. They really work.

Try to view the interview as an exhilarating experience rather than a stressful one. You could also think of it as a game.

You're going to be nervous. This can actually be a good thing if you can channel it into conveying energy and enthusiasm.

The key is to manage it. Don't continually say that you're nervous. They know you're nervous.

Time May Not Be on Your Side – Time Management in an Interview

The amount of time for an interview can vary quite a bit. In some cases, the interview will take 30 minutes, in others you may be involved in an all–day interview with many different groups of people. You'll even eat your meals with someone from the potential employer and these meals will be part of your evaluation.

In the public sector, the interviews are often short, running from about 30 minutes to 1.5 hours for the total time.

In many public sector interviews, the panel cannot change the amount of time for each candidate. If you take too long with one question, you won't be able to recover from this.

The actual interview, with a panel, usually runs about 50 minutes.

You will need to manage your time, or at least pay attention to the amount of time you use to answer each question.

Read the Question

In most cases you will be able to read all of the questions in advance, or at least when you sit down for the interview. Make sure to read the questions carefully so that you can budget you time appropriately for each question. For example, if there are 10 questions and the interview is scheduled for 1 hour, you should plan on talking about 5 minutes per question. If there is one question that you have a strong answer for, you can spend a little more time on that question and less on one for which you don't have as strong an answer.

Try to figure out what they want in each question. What's the category?

You also want to make sure you answer the question they ask. In one interview I actually missed one complete question because I was nervous enough that I didn't actually answer the question they asked. And as I've discussed, it's critical that you don't miss an entire question.

Leave Enough Time for Each Question

If you spend too long on an early question, you may run out of time for a later question which means that you would have not answered that question at all. This can strongly impact how you are evaluated or scored because you will get no points for one entire question. It won't matter that you had an awesome answer for one of the other questions if you miss a question. There are only so many points you may be awarded for any particular question. Refer to the section 3.5, It's the Math.

Take Your Time

It's been my experience that people are far more likely to rush through an interview and end it ahead of time rather than taking too long with any of the questions. If you budget your time appropriately and slow yourself down, you are much less likely to finish too fast. Answering questions as behavioral interview questions often helps with providing a longer, more descriptive

177

answer to an interview question. Refer to Section 4.4 for more information about behavioral interviewing.

Given that you are likely to be nervous and talk more quickly, slowing down will generally be a good thing. You are also much less likely to ummm when you speak more slowly.

4.9 Technology Issues During an Interview

Assume Technology Will Fail When You Need It Most

A job interview is a classic example of this type of situation. You will need backups that you can use if technology doesn't work for you during the interview.

If you have to do a presentation, think about how you can set up more than one version of the presentation that you can access if your first option fails.

When I did a presentation for one job, I had multiple backups of that presentation.

I'd created the presentation as a website. I'd posted online and also brought it as a disk with the files for the site so that I could simply run it on a computer using a browser.

I had printouts of the sites. And, because this was a while ago, I'd also brought along overhead slides that I could show using an overhead projector. I had 4 different versions of the same information.

Don't Panic When There Are Problems

It's also important to think about how you'll react if the technology fails. You should still be able to continue, even if something isn't working. A candidate who seems to "freeze" if there is a technical difficulty will not score highly for the interview for several reasons. For example, I'll wonder how they'll do on the job when technology fails. And I'll wonder why they didn't prepare for this.

Clear Your Desktop, Folders, and USB Drive

We often end up with a selection of random files and folders displayed on our computers. You will need to make sure these are all filed away before the interview. You'll avoid embarrassing surprises here such as inappropriate content or preparation for other interviews. If you are interviewing for multiple jobs you don't want your preparation materials for one organization to be visible to any others.

4.10 The End of the Interview

At the end of the interview you should be asked if you have anything else to add and if you have any questions to ask. Note that this is a two-part question and as with everything else about your interview, you should be prepared for this.

Sell Yourself One More Time – It's the last thing the panel will remember about you.

Always take this as an opportunity to sell yourself and leave the panel with a few positive things to remember you by. What are the 3–5 qualities you want them to remember.

Once again you should summarize why you would be an excellent addition to the organization in this position. Your answer should include a short summary of what you covered in the first question ("tell us a little bit about yourself"), and should highlight how well you would fit this position in terms of personality, skills and experience.

"I would like to say again that I would be an excellent fit for this position. I love your organization. I am good at .... I have these skills... I have this (applicable) experience... I am a hard worker and I would work well as a member of your team. I really appreciate this opportunity."

Always Thank the Panel

Participating on an interview panel takes a lot of time from schedules that are already busy. Honor that time commitment by thanking the panel.

You want to leave them with a positive impression.

You'll leave a much more positive impression if you thank everyone.

If the panel has not already informed you, you can ask about what will happen next in the process. If they have already informed you,

you can mention that that was your first question but you'd also like to (ask an additional question).

End of Interview Questions

You should always have questions prepared to ask a potential employer at the end of an interview. You should not be able to find these answers on their websites. Those are questions you should have already figured out when you're researching the organization before submitting your application and before the interview.

You should have more than one question ready to go in case your first choice of question won't work for some reason. For example, if they tell you about what the daily duties will be, you wouldn't want to ask a question relating to that.

General Examples:

• What is a typical day like in this position? Or you can ask the panel what a typical day is like for a couple of members of the panel. You can ask other questions of them based on their answers.
• How much guidance or assistance is made available to individuals in developing career goals?
• If I were to start tomorrow, what would you want me to start working on?
• What are the options for additional training and continuing education within this organization?
• I was looking at the website for your organization and I noticed that you do a lot of ..., what have been the benefits of this ...?
• It can be hard to get a full sense of the culture of an organization from the outside. What can you tell me about your organization from the perspective of an insider?
• What can you tell me about the team I might be working with?
• Why do you enjoy working for this organization?
• What is the company's policy on providing seminars, workshops, and training so employees can keep up their skills or acquire new ones?
• How will this position be evaluated?

- How does this organization communicate? Are there regular staff meetings?
- If I were to complete some professional development activities to fill a need you have, what would you recommend that I do?

What's your favorite part of your job?

This is a personal favorite of mine. It leaves the interview on a positive note. Additionally, if the interviewer or panel has a hard time with this or stammers a bit, that's an indication that there might be problems with this workplace. If people are happy in their jobs, they should be able to come up with an answer quickly and easily.

Post Interview

As soon as possible after you are done, take notes. For example: who was there, what questions were asked?

Don't forget to write thank you notes. Get the names of everyone who interviewed you. You may need to ask the receptionist for this information or call back later if you didn't remember to do it when you were there. Make sure to spell all names correctly.

4.11 What Ifs – Common Concerns About Interviewing

These are common worries about interviewing that I've heard from a variety of different people.

What If You Don't Know/Have a Skill in a Question?

Never start with "I don't know how to do....", "I've never done...."

People may tune out the rest of your answer if you start it with a negative statement.

Instead, start with a related positive idea, for example with any similar skills and/or experience that you have.

Let's look at how this works.

For many skills, even if you have not performed a task, you have experienced it. For example, even if you have never trained anyone, you have been trained. You can talk about good training experiences you've had, what you learned from that experience and how you might apply it on the job.

Talk about your ability to learn quickly and any previous situations where this has been important.

Talk about the process you would use or the steps you might take to try to figure things about. For example, you could say I'd ask for help from a coworker, I'd do research, I'd Google it, I'd check YouTube.

Finally, after you discuss the positive ways in which you match or meet this requirement you can acknowledge that you lack the skills or experience and your plan for mastering the skill. Make sure to mention any educational plans you have to address this need.

For example, "I'm planning on taking a class in Excel to make sure I've mastered that program at a more advanced level."

What If You Don't Know the Vocabulary in the Question?

Even if you are well prepared for your interview, and have done research and are familiar with the organization and position for which you are applying, you may be given an interview question with vocabulary that you don't recognize. This can happen to anyone.

Here's the strategy I suggest that you use in this situation.

Don't try to guess the meaning of the unknown word or phrase. If you guess incorrectly, you will give the wrong answer and receive no points for that entire question. As I mentioned in section 3.5 It's the Math, it's extremely important that you get at least a few points for each question. Zero points for any of the questions will really impact your overall interview score and ability to get the job, even if you do well with all of the other questions.

Instead of guessing, ask for a definition of the unknown vocabulary.

"I want to make sure I understand what .... is. Can you please tell me?"

Once you know the vocabulary, you may actually be able to answer the question correctly. You may know the word or phrase and have simply forgotten it during the interview. Or you may be able to talk about related knowledge or skills sets. Asking for the vocabulary will give you more options and you may even do really well with that question. Most importantly though, you will lose fewer points for asking what the vocabulary means than for giving a completely wrong answer.

Ask for a definition. It gives you more options.

You're always better off asking what a word or phrase means rather than trying to fake it. If you try to fake it and answer the question incorrectly you will have completely blown that question. If you ask what the vocabulary means you may actually be familiar with the topic and be able to provide an answer, or you may have parallel skills that will work.

185

"I want to make sure that I completely understand, can you please explain what it means."

However sometimes you really don't know the answer.

If you are asked about a situation for which you really have no idea how to answer it try not to freak out.

Be careful about the amount of detail you provide and going off on the wrong track.

Try to give a minimal answer and move on to the next question.

These would be really specific situational questions. For example, in a library setting you might be asked about how you would handle various patron interactions.

If you don't have any experience with this you need to be careful.

What If There's a Question About the Latest Trends in My Profession?

Do your research. Review the organization's website carefully.

Look at other similar positions for clues about what this type of position entails. You might find duties listed for another position that aren't listed on the one for which you are applying.

Find current conference programs from the field and see what people are doing presentations on. Sometimes you can find slides or videos from conference presentations.

Search on Twitter and other social media.

Search for videos to watch.

Use research databases to try to find articles on relevant topics.

What If I Know Someone on the Panel?

There are often situations in your professional life where you'll interview with someone you already know.

This is particularly true if you have done a lot networking, as you should be doing. I've been on many interview panels where I know at least one of the interview candidates. When this is the case, I always hope that they will pretend that they don't know me. This is your best strategy in this situation.

If you already know a person or several people on an interview panel, pretend that you've never met any of them before. Treat them as you treat everyone else that you are meeting for the first time at the interview.

This doesn't mean that you're rude to anyone or completely ignore them. You want to be pleasant and treat them as you treat anyone else.

There are several reasons why you should employ this strategy.

If you pretend that everyone is a stranger, you won't focus on the one person you already know because you're comfortable with them. Sometimes when people already are already acquainted with someone, they focus all of their energy on that person. You need to address everyone on the panel.

You also won't be overly relaxed. Your energy will be up and you will hopefully have that good type of nervous energy. Remember, everyone is nervous when they interview. The key is managing your nervousness so that you can still answer all of the questions well.

Another reason to treat everyone like a stranger is that you won't forget to talk about something because you think that any of the panel are already familiar with your work. Remember that with public sector interviews, whether or not you are hired is completely based on the interview. You will be less likely to see yourself through their eyes, which can be distracting and derailing.

4.12 Public Sector Interviewing

As I've mentioned several times throughout this book, it's been my experience that many people are unaware of the differences between public sector and private sector hiring and how this can affect their application and interview.

Public sector hiring is different than private sector hiring because it is controlled by equity, i.e. everyone is treated the same way.

Most public agencies go to great lengths to ensure that the process is equitable and fair to all candidates.

In order to make sure that all applicants are treated the same there are strict processes that govern everything.

This generally causes a higher level of bureaucracy.

The applications must be screened the same way. Interviews must be conducted the same way.

For public sector jobs you will literally be scored on your application and your interview. Make sure to read section 3.5 to see why understanding a little math is really important in this context.

The Interview

If you have a strong application and you're screened in, you will receive a call to come in for an interview.

When the employer contacts you to set up the interview, they will tell you what the format will be.

You should ask how many people are on the interview panel when you are contacted to schedule your interview. You will need this information to know how many copies of your resume or other handouts or work portfolios you should bring with you to the interview. If they give you an option, select a time slot (see section 4.3). Some time slots are better than others.

The Effect of Equity on the Interview

The interview is strongly affected by the principle of equity. I've heard people describe private sector interviews as a conversation. Public sector interviews will not follow this format. Because of their formality and structure, they can seem somewhat off-putting.

Here are a few specifics to keep in mind.

You will not be asked follow up questions. This means you have to express everything in your answers without any prompting from the interviewer(s).

This is why learning how to answer in a behavioral format is important with public sector interviewing. It provides a structure for you to talk about yourself that will give enough detail and information for your answers to shine. You'll find information on behavioral interviewing in section 4.4.

If you can't answer a question the panel will not help you because they have to treat all of the candidates the same way.

You may not receive feedback either formal or informal from the panel on how you're doing. The most extreme version I encountered of the lack of feedback from the panel was like talking into a void. But if you're prepared and aware of this format you can still do really well and get the job. I did. Make sure to smile even if the panel is not smiling.

Once you have made it to the interview, the only criteria which you are being judged is how well you do in the interview.

Just the interview. Not your application or that wonderful volunteer work you do (unless you work it into one of your interview answers).

It doesn't matter how beautiful your resume was. It doesn't matter if people on the panel already know you and wish to hire you.

You have to do well on the interview to get the job. If you blow the interview, you won't get the job, no matter what your credentials are.

Public Sector Format

Most public sector interviews are conducted by a panel. The size of the panel can vary. Most panels will consist of two to three people. However, there are many jobs where the panel may include six to nine people. I've been interviewed by a nine-person panel and heard of higher numbers. Be prepared for this.

Not everyone who is on the panel will have seen your application materials before the interview. Some of the panel will have screened your application, but some won't. You need to make sure to mention any relevant points during the interview. Remember, the interview is what controls whether you will be hired.

Once you arrive at the interview, you may be given time to review the interview questions before you go in for the actual interview. You may even be allowed to make notes (although they may take these from you at the end of the interview).

Depending on the level of the position, you may be asked to complete a writing sample.

Most interviews will take an hour or less. Check out section 4.8 (The Actual Interview) for information on timing your answers.

Most public sector interviews happen at a table. The panel will be seated across from you, either be at the other end of the table or at another table.

A copy of the interview questions may be provided for review on the table in front of you.

Once you sit down and are comfortable (or at least as comfortable as you can be) and have reviewed the questions, the interview will start.

The panel will introduce itself and then begin to ask you the questions, one panelist at a time.

Remember to smile and make eye contact with each panelist as much as possible. I usually start with the panelist who asked the question and then work my way around the room.

Because you are actually being scored by the panel, they will be taking notes as you provide your answers. Don't worry when you see them taking copious notes, that's usually a good sign that they want to be able to remember everything that you said.

Don'ts

As with a regular interview, never ask questions about salary or benefits during the interview.

Thank You

As always, make sure to thank the panel for their time before you leave. Remember that the panel has probably been trapped in this room for a while. They've also sacrificed their time for the interview and not completed work they need to finish. A thank you is really important.

Guaranteed Questions

There are a few questions that will be included in any public sector interview. You should always be prepared for these.

• Tell Us a Little Bit About Yourself (TUALBAY) is usually the opening question. This is your best opportunity to sell yourself and provide useful examples from your work history. See section 4.5 for more information about how to answer this question.
• Diversity/equity – you won't find this in all public sector jobs, but I would expect it for any jobs dealing with the public or people. This is also covered in section 4.5
• Do you have anything else to add? Always take this opportunity to sell yourself one last time. This is also covered in section 4.5.

• Do you have any questions? You should have a few questions ready to ask at the end of every interview. See the section 4.10 for more information about how to answer end of interview questions.

4.13 Distance Interviewing – Video and/or Audio

Here are a few specific tips if you're doing an interview off-site.

Tips for Either Audio or Visual Interviews

You should prepare as you would for a regular interview. Read the previous sections of Chapter 4 for multiple interviewing tips.

As always, go the extra mile.

Introduce yourself by name when you start. Audio and video interviews are flatter than interviews in real life. Introducing yourself will make more of an impression and you will be more likely to stick in the memories of the interviewers.

Here are a few special things you should think about for interviewing from a geographical distance.

Have multiple backups ready to go in case of technology snafus. I will repeat this multiple times in this section because it's critical.

Make sure you can use your cell phone if necessary. It should be fully charged and/or plugged in if your battery doesn't retain a charge any more.

Take the time to connect to another location a few times from the place you'll be doing the interview to make sure your end of the connection works and that the connection speed is sufficient.

Don't Panic If There Are Problems

If the technology does fail in any way, remember to keep your cool and do your best. Don't panic. Everyone can relate to this scenario, we've all been there. Try to calmly deal with the issue and communicate what's happening immediately. When technology has failed on during interviews I've conducted, I am definitely paying attention to how well people handle the stress of the situation. For example, I usually care more about how you handle the extra stress than I care about your demonstration.

Give Yourself Extra Prep Time and Have a Backup Plan

Give yourself more preparation time for distance interviews because they will involve the added complication of technology. As I mentioned in section 3.4 (Technology Issues), technology works all of the time, said no one ever.

With any interviews that are dependent on technology, i.e. distance interviews, you need to have backup plans for everything.

As with a normal interview, you should be ready to go online about 10–15 minutes early.

Practice with the technology about a week in advance. Do a run through of any presentations using the technology that you'll need during the interview.

Test your technology at the same time as you'll be interviewing. You'll see if there are any bandwidth/connectivity or other issues that you may need to deal with.

Phone Interview – i.e. Audio Only

Before the interview, when you're setting up logistics, ask how many people you will be talking to.

You may need to prepare for a conference call with multiple interviewers on the call. Depending on the quality of the audio, it may be hard to hear what people are saying. Don't hesitate to pleasantly ask for people to repeat the interview questions. You don't want to mishear the question and completely blow it. As I discussed in section 3.5, the math won't be in your favor.

Set up a mirror so you can see your face and remember to smile. Telemarketers do this because people sound different when they are smiling.

Audio only interviews actually offer certain advantages to the interviewee. For example, as demonstrated in the photo below, you can have all sorts of materials laid out and/or a stress reduction assistant nearby that you can use during the interview. You can't do that when you're interviewing in person.

Video Interviewing

Video interviewing is becoming increasingly common and these trends will continue. As of 2018, "video technology is being used by 60% of hiring managers and recruiters."[23]

Here are my suggestions for completing the best video interview possible.

Ask a good friend who will notice things to give you feedback ahead of time.

Technology Setup

Assume that technology might fail and plan accordingly. You should have multiple backups to connect and for any presentations you'll be doing. If all else fails, make sure you have a contact number for someone on the interview team. If the video fails, plan to do an audio interview.

Check your sound levels ahead of time.

Make sure that you have a stable surface for your computer or phone that won't vibrate. Camera movement will be really distracting to your interviewers.

Place your computer high enough so that the camera is slightly above eye level.

Because you'll be looking up a little bit, your eyes will appear to be open wider and you'll look better on screen.

You should get a keyboard and mouse for the table level to make it easier to operate your computer while it's above eye level.

Your setup doesn't have to be fancy. You can see my highly technical setup in the photo below.

Notice it's next to a window for good light. I also have a selfie light to ensure I have good lighting no matter where I am.

Online Interview Kit

• Power cords and/or batteries for all electronic devices.
• Pen and paper to take notes.
• Water or a similar beverage in a closed container (it won't spill).
• No ice, it's too noisy. Additionally, I often chew ice and I wouldn't want to forget and start crunching during the interview.
• Copy of the position description, your resume and cover letter. Using a big font will make it easy to read.
• Tissues
• Selfie light to make sure you're well lit
• Headphones – they may allow you to better hear the audio. Pro-tip – if you're using headphones that have a cord, string the cord behind your shoulder so it won't be visible.

Good Lighting Is Key

Natural lighting from a window is your best option. It's more even and usually nice and bright.

If you're using natural light make sure to test your setup at the same time of day as the interview.

However, if you don't have an interview spot that has good lighting, it would be worth it to invest in a selfie–light. They are readily available for about $20.

Regardless of which option you use, make sure your face is evenly lit from the front.

Light from above or below is not flattering and light behind you will make you look like someone who's in a witness protection program.

Your Background Is Your Interview Outfit

Remove background distractions. Turn off any noise making devices, such as stereo, TV, etc.

Turn off any ceiling fans. They're distracting and the motion will cause problems with your video quality.

Avoid spinning office chairs. If you are nervous, you might swing back and forth which is quite distracting.

If you will be visible on screen during the interview you should practice with someone who can honestly tell you how everything looks from the other end. This includes your outfit, your background, your technology and connection.

Check your background ahead of time. Things that look fine in reality may not present well on screen. I'd try for a clean desk with a neutral background. If you don't have a neutral background, make one happen. You could hang up a sheet, see what it looks like. Temporarily hang a nice work of art behind you. Ask for advice on how it looks.

You can use a virtual background if you don't have a good space to interview. Make sure to choose something neutral such as a nature scene. If you are sure of your audience, choose something appealing. For example, if you're interviewing for a library job, you could select an image with books or a famous library.

Put any pets or children in another room while you are interviewing if possible.

Your Interview Outfit and Display

Check for shiny nose and face. Regardless of gender you need to make sure your nose isn't shiny. It will be distracting. It's another reason to check your setup ahead of time. You can see what your face looks like on camera.

Clothes

Clothes are not as important with video interviews because you don't actually see that much of your clothing, generally just the collar of your shirt and a little bit lower. I have noticed that lighter and brighter shirt colors are more visible and display a little better.

However, even though most of your outfit won't be visible on screen, you need to dress as you would for an in-person interview.

You will behave differently if you are formally dressed, than you would if you're wearing pajamas. This is true even if you're doing a completely audio interview with no visuals.

Additionally, if something happens and your entire outfit were to suddenly appear on screen because of unforeseeable circumstances, you don't want to be wearing something that would be embarrassing.

Never, Ever, Ever

- Smoke
- Eat or drink alcoholic beverages
- Complete personal grooming such as combing your hair, brushing your teeth, or trimming your nails
- Answer your cell phone (unless it seems to be a complete emergency)
- Do housework or walk your dog (particularly during audio–only interviews.
- Multi–task other things – be completely present or the interview. You need to actively listen to everything.

Remember to Breath

As with an in–person interview, remember to breathe and remain calm. You might want to read section 4.2 for more tips to de–stress. Virtual interviews will still be highly stressful.

Don't Forget to Thank Everyone

Make sure to thank them at the end before you end the interview.

Then send thank you notes ASAP. You'll find more about thank you note etiquette in section 3.10.

Chapter 5 – If You're Buying This Book for an Interview Tomorrow or You Just Want to See the Best Tips from this Book

These are the top tips and tricks for job hunting from this book.

General Tips

Do a little research about the company or organization. (section 1.3)

Assume that technology may fail at any time. Always have backups. (sections 3.4, 4.13)

Network, network, network. (Chapter 2)

Join LinkedIn and put your LinkedIn URL on your business cards. (section 2.2)

Resume and Cover Letter

Get a Gmail address with some version of your name for job hunting. (section 3.4)

Use a T style cover letter. (section 3.8)

Resume: choose a good font, get rid of italics, bold the job title, no objective, list 5 qualities you'd like to emphasize. (sections 3.7)

Interviewing

Review the job ad to figure out the categories of questions you're likely to get. (section 1.4)

Do the Power Posz. (section 4.3)

Slow Your Breathing. (section 4.7)

Remember to smile. (section 4.8)

Avoid the ums. (section 4.8)

Indicate that you want to work for that specific company or organization. (section 1.3)

Be prepared for Behavioral Interviewing and telling stories about yourself. (section 4.4)

Have answers ready for the strengths and weaknesses questions. (section 4.5)

Always ask end of interview questions. (section 4.10)

Thank people for their time. (section 4.10)

Write thank you notes or emails. (section 3.10)

Learn how to ace video or audio Interviews. (section 4.13)

Learn specifics about public sector hiring. (sections 3.5, 4.12)

Record what you remember of the interview for next time. (section 4.10)

Review common interview questions and categories (Appendix)

Read the rest of this book when you have time.

Appendix - Interview Questions

This is a long list of interview questions that I've collected over time and organized into common categories. Remember, you should be prepared for the category of the question, rather than preparing to answer specific questions.

Some of the questions have been listed in several categories. This is to show the possible emphasis you may want to use to answer the question.

For example, "What is your dream job?" could be answered to market yourself and highlight your skills, talk about previous experience, talk about your goals and future plans and intellectual interests, just to name a few.

I highly recommend checking the site Mock Questions (https://www.mockquestions.com) for specific questions from different professions. They provide excellent examples of questions and suggest possible answers you might want to use.

General Questions

Most of these questions are a version of "Tell Us a Little Bit About Yourself" (TUALBAY).

Refer to section 4.5 (Written Interview Preparation – Beyond STAR for suggestions about how to answer this most common of interview questions.

- How would you describe yourself?
- How are you qualified for this job?
- If you were hiring someone for this job, what qualities would you look for?
- Please describe your ideal job.
- Please tell us a little bit about yourself. Why are you interested in this position?
- Tell me about yourself –– why did you choose this type of work?
- What appeals to you about this position?

- What are some of the things on your jobs that you feel you have done particularly well?
- What are the personal characteristics and qualities that you would bring to this position that would be particularly helpful in fulfilling the responsibilities of this position?
- What does success mean to you? How do you judge it?
- What experience do you have that you feel qualifies you for this position?
- What interests you about this job?
- What is your dream job?
- What kind of work environment do you prefer?
- While this position involves some specific skills (language, computer, cataloging, etc.), it is more of a generalist position. How do you feel that your background fits into this?
- Why did you choose to major in...?
- Why did you decide to apply for this position?
- Why do you want this job?
- Why do you want to move to this area?
- Why do you want to work for us?

Definitely be prepared to discuss a situation or experience that went poorly.

Adaptability

- Are you a big picture person or detail-oriented person? Why? Can you give an example that demonstrates this?
- Do you prefer to work on the details of a project, or would you rather pass those tasks on to a co-worker?
- Are you a person who likes to "try new things," or "stay with regular routines"? Give an example.
- In this position you will be on your own for much of the time, please describe your experience working alone and your experiences working with others.
- The person in this position needs to be innovative and proactive. Can you describe some things you have done to demonstrate these qualities?

Attention to Detail

• Are you a big picture person or detail-oriented person? Why? Can you give an example that demonstrates this?
• Do you prefer to work on the details of a project, or would you rather pass those tasks on to a co-worker?
• How do you ensure quality when you're under a time constraint?
• How do you find errors that aren't immediately obvious?
• How do you keep track of all the tasks you need to complete for a project?
• Please describe a situation where you made an error and didn't catch it. How did you handle it? How did you find out?
• Tell us about a situation where attention to detail was either important or unimportant in accomplishing an assigned task.
• What do you do in order to prevent mistakes?
• What tools and methods do you use to check your work?

Communication Skills

• How would you rate your communication skills and what have you done to improve them?
• In this position you will be on your own for much of the time, please describe your experience working alone and your experiences working with others.
• Please describe skills and methods you would use to communicate with coworkers.
• Some people get to know strangers quickly, while others prefer to take their time letting people get to know them. Describe how you entered relationships when you were "new" on a job.
• Tell us about a time when you had to tell a superior something unpleasant, and how did you go about it?
• This position involves public speaking. Please tell us about your experiences in public speaking and with teaching classes.
• What does the term two-way communication mean to you? When have you successfully used two-way communication?
• What would you do if you were trying to explain a concept to a coworker and they were not understanding it?

• What experience do you have with training other staff members?

Creativity and Problem Solving

• Describe a situation where you had to solve a problem. How did you do it?
• How do you handle a task that seems to be impossible?
• How did you cope with change in the workplace---what was it, and what did you do?
• If you could solve any problem in the world, what would it be?
• In this position you will be on your own for much of the time, please describe your experience working alone and your experiences working with others.
• Tell us about a situation in which you had a difficult relationship with a co-worker; what exactly was the situation, and how did you handle it?
• The person in this position needs to be innovative and proactive. Can you describe some things you have done to demonstrate these qualities?
• What did you do the last time you were unsure of a work-related decision?
• What would you do if you were unsure about how to accomplish a task you were given at work?
• What would you do if you won 10 million dollars?

Equity, Diversity, and Anti-Racism

Read section 4.5 for information about how to answer this type of question.

• Explain how diversity has played a role in your career.
• Has diversity played a role in shaping your teaching and advising styles?
• Have you done any work in the area of diversity in the community?
• How have you handled a situation when a colleague was not accepting of others' diversity?

- How have you participated in diversity events and organizations at the other colleges and universities?
- How would you work with people to foster a climate receptive to diversity in the workforce, in the curriculum, in faculty/staff meetings?
- In what ways have you integrated multicultural issues as part of your professional development?
- Tell me about a time you had to alter your work style to meet a diversity need or challenge?
- Tell the committee about a time that you successfully adapted to a culturally different environment?
- Tell the committee about a time when you had to adapt to a wide variety of people by accepting/understanding their perspectives?
- What books/materials/authors have you read on the subject of diversity and anti-racism?
- What do you see as the most challenging aspect of a diverse working environment? What steps have you taken to meet this challenge?
- What do you see as the most challenging aspects of an increasingly diverse academic community?
- Follow-up question: What initiatives have you taken in your previous capacities to meet such challenges?
- What does it mean to have a commitment to diversity and how would you develop and apply your commitment at this company?
- What efforts have you made, or been involved with, to foster diversity competence and understanding?
- What have you done to further your knowledge/understanding about diversity? How have you demonstrated your learning?
- What is your vision of diversity in our organization?
- What kinds of experiences have you had working with others with different backgrounds than your own?
- What strategies have you used to address diversity challenges? What were the positives and negatives?
- What was/is the diversity value at your current/former employer? What impact did you make on this value?

Goals, Future Plans, and Motivation

- Do you do personal planning? If so, what are your goals?
- Do you plan to continue your education?
- What are some of the thing you are either doing now or have thought about doing that are self-development activities?
- What do you see yourself doing five or ten years from now?
- What important goals have you set in the past, and how successful have you been in working toward their accomplishment?
- What is your dream job?
- What kind of position are you looking for when you graduate?
- Where do you see yourself going from here?

Intellectual Interests

- Are there any podcasts you would recommend?
- What are your hobbies?
- What are you watching?
- What courses (high school/college) did you find most satisfying? Least satisfying? Why?
- What do you like to do in your spare time?
- What have you read lately, and what are you reading now?
- What is your dream job?

Management and Supervision Experience

Remember, even if you haven't supervised anyone, you been supervised.
Even if you haven't trained anyone, you have been trained.
Make sure to include how you communicate with your team as part of your answer. Communication is foundational to managing and supervising.

- Describe a need you saw in a previous position and what steps you took to fill that need.
- Describe a time when you were under pressure to make a decision. Did you react immediately or take time in deciding what to do?

• Discuss how you handle conflict in a work environment.

• How would you characterize your supervisory style?

• Some people have the ability to "step into another's shoes." When has this skill been required of you?

• Tell us about a time when you had to tell a superior something unpleasant, and how did you go about it?

• The person in this position needs to be innovative and proactive. Can you describe some things you have done to demonstrate these qualities?

• What experience do you have with training other staff members?

• What motivates you? Have you used these motivators with others?

• What supervisory experience have you had?

• What would you do to implement the provisions of some other new policy in our library, and how would you prioritize this among your other duties?

• Who or what in your life would you say influenced you most with regard to your career objectives?

Networking Strikes Again – Familiarity with the Organization

You should have done research about the organization and come up with specific questions you can ask. This is yet another area where Networking Strikes Again. If you know someone on the inside, you can really tailor these questions to demonstrate that you've done your homework.

• Do you have any questions about our organization?

• What do you know about our library? university? community? company?

• You have just had a short tour of this organization. Did any aspect or anything you saw or heard surprise you?

People Skills and Customer Service

• Customers frequently create a great deal of pressure. What has been your experience in this area?

• Describe a problem person you have had to deal with. What did you say or do?

• Discuss how you handle conflict in a work environment.

• Dishonesty in the workplace: describe a situation of discovering dishonesty/stealing, and how did you handle it?

• Do you prefer working alone or in groups?

• Give an example of a group project you worked on and how you participated.

• Give an example of a time you dealt successfully with an angry customer, and also a time when you provided excellent customer service.

• How do you react when you see co-workers disagreeing? Do you become involved or hold back?

• How do you work in groups, and what experience have you had working in groups?

• In this position you will be on your own for much of the time, please describe your experience working alone and your experiences working with others.

• Please tell us how you deal with customers who are indignant.

• Some people get to know strangers quickly, while others prefer to take their time letting people get to know them. Describe how you entered relationships when you were "new" on a job.

• Tell about how you establish a rapport with a kind of patron unfamiliar to you.

• Tell us about a situation in which you had a difficult relationship with a co-worker. What exactly was the situation and how did you handle it?

• Tell us about a time when you had to tell a superior something unpleasant, and how did you go about it?

• What experience do you have with training other staff members?

• What have been your experiences in dealing with the general public? When have people really tried your patience?

• What is your idea of good customer service?

209

- What kind of people do you like to work with?
- What kind of people do you find it most difficult to work with? What do you do to improve the situation?
- What types of experiences have you had in dealing with difficult customers?
- What would you do if you were trying to explain a concept to a coworker and they were not understanding it?
- What would you do if you were unsure how to handle a work situation?

Professional Development (How Are You Keeping Up?)

- Have you completed any coursework recently that would update your skills? Please explain what it is and why you took it.
- How do you keep up with changes in technology?
- How do you keep up with changes in the profession?
- What conferences have you attended?
- What industry social media and websites do you read on a regular basis?
- What professional groups are you a member of, and how active have you been in those groups?

Responsibility

- Do you prefer to have a job in which you have well laid out tasks and responsibilities, or one in which your work changes on a frequent basis?
- How do you handle a task that seems to be impossible?
- How has your present job developed you to take on even greater responsibilities?
- In your current position what types of decisions do you make without consulting your immediate supervisor?
- Tell us about a task that was a challenge.
- Tell us about a time when you asked for extra responsibility for your job.
- What did you do the last time you were unsure of a work–related decision?

Strengths

Read section 4.5 for information about how to answer this type of question.

If you are having trouble coming up with your strengths, you might want to try to answer a few of these questions. Your answers should provide you with some ideas about what your strengths are.

- Describe your most rewarding experience.
- In what ways do you think you can make a contribution to our department?
- In what kind of work environment are you most comfortable?
- List three of your most important/proudest accomplishments.
- Some people have the ability to "step into another's shoes." When has this skill been required of you?
- Starting with your last job, would you tell me about some of your achievements that were recognized by your superiors?
- What are some aspects of your present position that you like?
- What are some of the things on your jobs that you feel you have done particularly well?
- What are some of your likes and dislikes about previous jobs?
- What are the personal characteristics and qualities that you would bring to this position that would be particularly helpful in fulfilling the responsibilities of this position?
- What are your strengths and weaknesses?
- What do you like to do in your spare time?
- What does success mean to you? How do you judge it?
- What else besides your school and job experience qualifies you for this job?
- What has been your greatest achievement?
- What kinds of things do you feel most confident in doing?
- What motivates you to put forth your best effort?
- What qualifications do you have that make you think you will be a success at this job?
- What things give you the greatest satisfaction?

• What two or three accomplishments have given you the most satisfaction? Why?

• What would you say there is about you that has accounted for your fine progress to date?

• Why do you think this organization should hire you?

• Why would you do well in this job?

• You mentioned you enjoyed your last job. What did you enjoy most? Least?

Technology

• Can you install software on computers and perform basic maintenance on them?

• Do you have the skills necessary to create and maintain our home pages?

• How to you keep up with changes in technology?

• How would you explain a computer concept to a novice computer user?

• How would you explain a computer concept to an experienced computer user?

• If you had to choose one program to do all of your work, which one would it be and why?

• If you woke up and had 2,000 emails, but could only answer 300, how would you handle it?

• Please tell us how you would turn a wireless card on for both a Mac and a PC.

• Tell us about your experience with [name of technology].

• What are your favorite apps?

• What are your favorite programs?

• What is your experience with using social media?

• Which computer programs are you familiar with?

Time Management Skills

• Describe how you determined your priorities on your last job.
• Describe how you schedule your time on an unusually hectic day. Give a specific example.
• How did you organize your work in your last position? What happened to your plan when emergencies came up?
• If you have a long list of tasks to accomplish, how to you proceed and prioritize those tasks?
• If you woke up and had 2,000 emails, but could only answer 300, how would you handle it?
• In this position you will be on your own for much of the time, please describe your experience working alone and your experiences working with others.
• When you have a lot of work to do, how do you get it all done? Give me an example.

Weaknesses

Read section 4.5 for information about how to answer this type of question.

As with the strengths section, if you are having trouble coming up with your weaknesses, you might want to try to answer a few of these questions. Your answers should provide you with some ideas about what they are

• Describe your least rewarding work experience.
• Give an example of when you got difficult feedback from a manager, customer, etc. How did you handle it?
• How did you cope with change in the workplace? What was it, and what did you do?
In what kind of work environment are you most comfortable?
• Please tell us about a work situation that did not go as well as you would have liked.
• Tell me about a time when you had work problems or stresses that were difficult for you. What did you do?

- Tell us about a situation in which you had a difficult relationship with a co-worker; what exactly was the situation, and how did you handle it?
- What are some of the problems you encounter in doing your job? Which one frustrates you the most? What do you usually do about it?
- What are some of the things about your last job that you found difficult to do?
- What are some things you would like to avoid in a job? Why?
- What did you enjoy least about your last job?
- What kinds of things do you feel somewhat less confident in doing?
- What traits or qualities do you feel could be strengthened or improved?
- What types of pressures do you experience on your current job? How do you cope with these pressures?
- What types of things make you angry? How do you react?
- What will your last supervisor tell me are your two weakest areas?
- What are some aspects of your present position that you dislike?
- What are some of your likes and dislikes about previous jobs?
- You mentioned you enjoyed your last job. What did you enjoy most? Least?

Notes

[1] McGonigal, Jane. *The Game That Can Give You 10 Extra Years of Life.* 2012. *www.ted.com,* https://www.ted.com/talks/jane_mcgonigal_the_game_that_can_give_you_10_extra_years_of_life. Accessed 5 July 2020.

[2] Bolles, Richard N. *What Color Is Your Parachute 2014: A Practical Manual for Job-Hunters and Career-Changers.* 2013th ed., Ten Speed Press, 2018.

[3] *2019 Hiring Statistics, Trends & Data: The Ultimate List of Recruitment Stats - Jobbatical. jobbatical.com,* https://jobbatical.com/resources/hiring-statistics. Accessed 5 July 2020.

[4] "Hidden Job Market." *Nostetta Urallesi,* 12 Nov. 2013. *rekrytointi.com,* https://rekrytointi.com/tyonhaku/en/working-in-finland/hidden-job-market. Accessed 5 July 2020.

[5] Adler, Lou. *New Survey Reveals 85% of All Jobs Are Filled Via Networking* | *LinkedIn.* 28 Feb. 2016, https://www.linkedin.com/pulse/new-survey-reveals-85-all-jobs-filled-via-networking-lou-adler. Accessed 5 July 2020.

[6] Schneider, Michael. "7 LinkedIn Statistics That Will Make You Question Your Recruitment Strategy." *Inc.Com,* 14 June 2018. *www.inc.com,* https://www.inc.com/michael-schneider/7-linkedin-hiring-trends-that-will-change-way-you-recruit.html. Accessed 5 July 2020.

[7] LinkedIn Talent Solutions, "The Ultimate List of Hiring Statistics for Hiring Managers, HR Professionals, and Recruiters." *Ultimate-List-of-Hiring-Stats-V02.04.Pdf.* https://business.linkedin.com/content/dam/business/talent-solutions/global/en_us/c/pdfs/Ultimate-List-of-Hiring-Stats-v02.04.pdf. Accessed 5 July 2020.

[8] "About LinkedIn." "About LinkedIn." *LinkedIn,* 2020. *about.linkedin.com,* https://about.linkedin.com. Accessed 5 July 2020.

[9] The Muse. "Your LinkedIn Intervention: 5 Changes You Must Make." *Forbes*, 6 July 2012. *www.forbes.com*, https://www.forbes.com/sites/dailymuse/2012/07/06/your-linkedin-intervention-5-changes-you-must-make. Accessed 5 July 2020.

[10] Nyman, Tina. "Your LinkedIn Profile Picture Matters More than You Think." *Medium*, 5 Oct. 2017. *medium.com*, https://medium.com/fallup/your-linkedin-profile-picture-matters-more-than-you-think-2faf21a2bd63. Accessed 22 June 2020.

[11] Abbott, Lydia. *10 Tips for Picking the Right LinkedIn Profile Picture.* 5 Aug. 2019. *business.linkedin.com*, http://talent.linkedin.com/blog/index.php/2014/12/5-tips-for-picking-the-right-linkedin-profile-picture. Accessed 5 July 2020.

[12] Nyman, Tina. "Your LinkedIn Profile Picture Matters More than You Think." *Medium*, 5 Oct. 2017. *medium.com*, https://medium.com/fallup/your-linkedin-profile-picture-matters-more-than-you-think-2faf21a2bd63. Accessed 22 June 2020.

[13] Nyman, Tina. "Your LinkedIn Profile Picture Matters More than You Think." *Medium*, 5 Oct. 2017. *medium.com*, https://medium.com/fallup/your-linkedin-profile-picture-matters-more-than-you-think-2faf21a2bd63. Accessed 22 June 2020.

[14] *JobStar--What Is a Resume?* http://jobstar.org/tools/resume/res-def.php. Accessed 22 June 2020.

[15] "The 6 Second Resume Challenge." *Resume Genius. resumegenius.com*, https://resumegenius.com/6-second-resume-challenge. Accessed 22 June 2020.

[16] Ronin, Kara. "How First Impressions Are Formed: The Psychology." *Executive Impressions*, 2 Mar. 2015. *www.executive-impressions.com*, http://www.executive-impressions.com/blog/not-waste-7-seconds-first-impression. Accessed 5 July 2020.

[17] Cuddy, Amy. *Your Body Language May Shape Who You Are.* 2012. *www.ted.com*, https://www.ted.com/talks/amy_cuddy_your_body_language_may_shape_who_you_are. Accessed 5 July 2020.

[18] Rudloff, Alex. *Complete List of Behavioral Interview Questions*. 21 May 2007, https://law.duke.edu/sites/default/files/images/career/Complete_List_o f_Behavioral_Interview_Questions_and_Answers.pdf. Accessed 5 July 2020.

[19] Petrova, Sasha. "Watching Cat Videos Lowers Stress And Makes You Happy, Study Suggests." *ScienceAlert*, 20 June 2015. *www.sciencealert.com*, https://www.sciencealert.com/watching-cat-videos-lowers-stress-and-makes-you-happy-study-reveals. Accessed 5 July 2020.

[20] "The Power of Cute: How Looking at Pictures of Baby Animals Can Help Improve Your Concentration Levels." *Mail Online*, 29 Sept. 2012. *www.dailymail.co.uk*, https://www.dailymail.co.uk/news/article-2210614/The-power-cute-How-looking-pictures-baby-animals-help-improve-concentration-levels.html. Accessed 5 July 2020.

[21] Vedantam, Shankar. "Why It's Not Too Late To Make A New Year's Resolution." *NPR.Org*, 19 Jan. 2016. *www.npr.org*, https://www.npr.org/2016/01/18/463220298/why-its-not-too-late-to-make-a-new-years-resolution. Accessed 5 July 2020.

[22] "To Clear Negative Thoughts, Physically Throw Them Away: Study." *HuffPost*, 7 Jan. 2013. *www.huffpost.com*, https://www.huffpost.com/entry/throw-away-negative-thoughts-trash_n_2205816. Accessed 5 July 2020.

[23] "Video Interviewing in 2018: Trends and Insights." *Talentnow RecruitX*, 2 Apr. 2018. *www.talentnow.com*, https://www.talentnow.com/video-interviewing-in-2018-trends-and-insights. Accessed 5 July 2020.

Acknowledgements

I wish to thank my husband and children, Steve, Madeline, and Charlotte. I couldn't do this without you.

Thanks to my parents, Helene and Gary Posz. You've enabled me to be the person I am. I appreciate all of the support and opportunities you provided to me. You've given me the tools and life skills to be successful and I love sharing them with others.

Thanks to my students. I always learn from you and am forever thankful that I have such an awesome job.

Thanks to my coworkers and fellow librarians. In particular I want to thank Terri Clark, Judy Howe, and Rebecca Goodchild who've all given me a lot of support and advice over the years.

Thanks to Kari Wergeland for the writing and publication advice. It's been invaluable.

And finally, thanks to Nicole Woolley, my work wife. You make my job so much more enjoyable. I'm so thankful we get to work together.

About the Author

As the daughter of a diplomat, Pamela Posz traveled the world in her childhood, with stops in Morocco, Los Angeles, Virginia, Alaska, Canada, India, New Zealand, and California.

All of those travels were a great background for majoring in Anthropology at the University of California, Davis, where she also majored in Art and worked at the campus library as a book shelver.

After graduation, she was fortunate enough to get a job at the Library of Congress in the Prints & Photographs Division where her interest in the library profession was solidified. After a few years, she attended graduate school and received her Master's in Library and Information Science from the University of Illinois.

After moving back to Sacramento and working in a variety of libraries in the area, she landed at Sacramento City College, where she's worked ever since. She enjoys being a librarian and running the Library and Information Technology Program where she has the pleasure of introducing students to the wonderful field of libraries and guide them into the workforce.

In her spare time, Pamela enjoys relaxing at home, making art, reading, and spending time with her family, as well as her 2 cats and 2 dogs.

Index